I0248299

GCSE
Success

REVISION GUIDE

German

Gavin Hillage

Contents

Leisure and Lifestyle (cont.)

Holidays and Travel

The Wider World

Vocabulary and Grammar

Exam Advice

Listening and Reading

All instructions and questions on both listening and reading papers are in English* and require your answers to be written in English*. Each test is worth 20% of the total marks, so your final listening and reading exams combined make up 40% of your grade. On foundation tier papers, examiners have to use the vocabulary lists printed in your exam specification. On higher tier papers there are additional words, printed in the exam specification, that you must learn; there will also be some unfamiliar words, which you should be able to work out the meaning of using communication strategies (see below). Many of the questions will be multiple choice, but other tasks – such as gap fill, matching exercises, answering in English and true / false / not mentioned (reading only) – will also be used. Here are some strategies for tackling these comprehension questions:

- Vocabulary is key. The more words you know, the easier the tests should be, so keep revising.
- Read the questions carefully before answering. Sometimes a single word can make a big difference. 'What food does he like?' and 'What food does he dislike?' need very different answers.
- Before the start of the listening test you will be given 5 minutes to read through the questions. Use this time sensibly: read carefully and think ahead of possible answers or vocabulary you think you will hear. Write notes on your test paper if necessary.
- Always use a black pen and make sure you form your letters and numbers clearly. Ensure your writing can be read. If you cross out an answer, write the new answer as close to the original as possible. Your papers will be scanned and marked online by people who are not used to your handwriting.

- Do not panic if you do not understand every word you read or hear. The key skill is to work out the gist. If the speaker sounds angry or if the text is full of negative words, then you can guess opinions. Use the other words you know to help you to understand the unfamiliar words.
- Never leave a blank space on your paper. Make an educated guess if you are stuck.
- Look out for negative expressions and time words, as these often catch students out.
- Do not assume the first word you hear is the correct answer. **Ich fahre nie mit dem Bus zur Schule, ich gehe zu Fuß** means that the speaker actually goes on foot, not by bus. Examiners love trying to catch you out like that.
- Recognising tenses is important. Listen or look for the verbs. Remember that the verbs could be at the end of sentences, so look there first.
- Revise high frequency words such as **oft**, **immer**, **nie**, **außer** and **manchmal** as they can alter the meaning of a sentence.
- Try to learn vocabulary in categories so that you can see the connections between words. If the answer to a question is 'reading', the word **lesen** may not appear at all. Words such as **ein Roman** (a novel) or **eine Zeitung** (a newspaper) might give you the answer instead.

*This may be in Welsh, depending on your exam board.

✓ Maximise Your Marks

You may have to use communication strategies to work out the meaning of some unfamiliar words used on higher tier papers. You may know that **spielen** means 'to play', so it is reasonable to expect you to know that **Spieler** is a 'player' and that **ein Spiel** is 'a game'.

◊ Boost Your Memory

Use brainstorming diagrams in your revision to help you visualise groups of words.

Speaking

The speaking part of your exam is worth 30% of the total mark and is tested through controlled assessments during your GCSE course. Your best pieces will be submitted to the exam board. These will be marked by your teacher. Each assessment should last between 4 and 6 minutes. Your teacher will give you a task and then you can plan what you want to say. Your teacher cannot help you at this stage. You are allowed a sheet with up to 30 or 40 words* on it to guide you as you complete the task. Ask your teacher what you can include on this.

- When planning your response, go through your notes and highlight language that you can recycle in your controlled assessment. It is likely that your prior classwork will be very useful.
- At the end of the task your teacher will ask you an additional question that you may not have prepared. The answer does not need to be a long one, but does need to contain a verb. When preparing for your task, you could guess what questions your teacher could ask you based on the topic and prepare possible answers.
- Make sure you give plenty of opinions and reasons why in your conversation.
- Include a variety of time frames, such as past, present, future and conditional tenses.
- Practise pronouncing words containing **ch**, **s**, **z**, **w**, **v** and vowels with an umlaut, i.e. **ä**, **ö** and **ü**.
- Avoid answers that are too short. Always try and develop what you say and add extra information.
- Make your sentences longer and more complex by using connectives such as **und**, **weil**, **obwohl** and **sobald** or by using relative pronouns.

*The exact number of words depends on your exam board. Check this with your teacher.

✓ Maximise Your Marks

You will get higher marks if you justify your opinions. This means always saying *why* you like or dislike something. Get in the habit of always adding **weil** and / or **obwohl** when you give an opinion. You could then develop your answer by saying what your friend / mum / rabbit likes and dislikes and give reasons. For example: **Ich esse gern Fleisch, weil es gesund ist, aber mein Vater isst kein Fleisch, weil er Vegetarier ist.**

Writing

The writing is also worth 30% of the total mark and is also tested through controlled assessments. Your two best pieces of writing done during your GCSE course will be submitted to the exam board. The exam board will mark these. Each assessment should be between 100 and 350 words*. Your teacher will give you a task and then you can plan what you want to say. Your teacher cannot help you at this stage. You are allowed a sheet with up to 30 or 40 words* on it to guide you as you complete the task. Ask your teacher what you can include on this.

- When planning your response, go through your notes and highlight language that you can recycle in your controlled assessment. It is likely that your prior classwork will be very useful.
- Use a variety of tenses in your work and include opinions, reasons and justifications wherever possible.
- Longer and more complex sentences always score more marks.
- You may use a dictionary. Check spellings and genders only. Do not be tempted to look up new words in the controlled assessment time, as you will be likely to make mistakes. The first word you see in the dictionary is never usually the word you need.
- Make use of adverbs, adjectives (check that the endings agree) and pronouns to make your work more personal and interesting. Write about somebody else now and again, rather than using **ich** all of the time.

*The exact number of words depends on your exam board. Check this with your teacher.

✓ Maximise Your Marks

Many questions at A* require you to structure your response logically in order to score maximum marks and also want you to give and explain different points of view. Narrating an event is also important for higher marks. This involves talking about a sequence of events. Use sequencers to help you with this: **erstens** (firstly), **zweitens** (secondly), **danach** (afterwards).

Basic German

Numbers

0	null	17	sieb**zehn**	50	fünfzig	first	ers**te**
1	eins	18	achtzehn	60	sech**zig**	second	zwei**te**
2	zwei	19	neunzehn	70	sieb**zig**	third	drit**te**
3	drei	20	zwanzig	80	achtzig	fourth	vier**te**
4	vier	21	einundzwanzig	90	neunzig	fifth	fünf**te**
5	fünf	22	zweiundzwanzig	100	hundert	twentieth	zwanzig**ste**
6	sechs	23	dreiundzwanzig	101	hunderteins	thirtieth	dreißig**ste**
7	sieben	24	vierundzwanzig	200	zweihundert		
8	acht	25	fünfundzwanzig	1000	tausend	1st	1.
9	neun	26	sechsundzwanzig	1 000 000	eine **M**illion	2nd	2.
10	zehn	27	siebenundzwanzig			3rd	3.
11	elf	28	achtundzwanzig	about 10	ungefähr zehn	4th	4.
12	zwölf	29	neunundzwanzig	about 30	ungefähr dreißig	5th	5.
13	dreizehn	30	drei**ß**ig			20th	20.
14	vierzehn	31	einunddreißig			30th	30.
15	fünfzehn	35	fünfunddreißig				
16	sech**zehn**	40	vierzig				

Days, Months and Seasons

die Woche	week
der Tag	day
Montag	Monday
Dienstag	Tuesday
Mittwoch	Wednesday
Donnerstag	Thursday
Freitag	Friday
Samstag / Sonnabend	Saturday
Sonntag	Sunday

Was für einen Tag haben wir heute?
What day is it today?

Heute ist Freitag der erste Mai.
Today is Friday the 1st of May.

Heute ist Dienstag der sechzehnte November.
Today is Tuesday the 16th of November.

das Jahr	year	**der Monat**	month
Januar	January	**Juli**	July
Februar	February	**August**	August
März	March	**September**	September
April	April	**Oktober**	October
Mai	May	**November**	November
Juni	June	**Dezember**	December

die Jahreszeit	season
der Frühling	spring
der Sommer	summer
der Herbst	autumn
der Winter	winter

✓ Maximise Your Marks

Make your work more interesting and include time words in your answers.

Use **am** to say 'on' a day:
- **Ich spiele am Montag Golf.**
  I'm playing golf on Monday.

Use **im** to say 'in' a month, a season or a year:
- **im Mai** in May
- **im Herbst** in autumn
- **im Jahr 2012** in 2012
- **Ich fahre im Mai nach Polen.**
  I'm travelling to Poland in May.

Never say 'in Mai' or 'in Sommer' or 'in 2012'.

Remember, if you start a sentence with a time word, the subject and verb swap places:

←→
- **Im Jahr 2013 werde ich die Schule verlassen.**
  In 2013 I will leave school.

Telling the Time

Understanding how to tell the time in German is important. Examiners love it.

die Zeit	the time
Wieviel Uhr ist es? / Wie spät ist es?	What time is it?

Es ist...	It is...
ein Uhr	one o'clock
zwei Uhr	two o'clock
fünf Uhr	five o'clock
einundzwanzig Uhr	9 p.m. / 21:00
fünf nach acht	five past eight
zehn nach acht	ten past eight
Viertel nach acht	quarter past eight
halb neun	half past eight (not nine!)
Viertel vor neun	quarter to nine
zehn vor neun	ten to nine
fünf vor neun	five to nine

✓ Maximise Your Marks

The 24-hour clock is used a lot by German speakers and is easier to form. Be prepared for this in your exam.

sieben Uhr dreizehn	07:13
zwölf Uhr vierzig	12:40
zweiundzwanzig Uhr fünfundzwanzig	22:25

💡 Boost Your Memory

Watch out for the word **halb**. German speakers say half *to* the hour: **halb zehn** means 'half *to* ten' (i.e. 'half past nine') *not* half past ten.

um	at
um dreizehn Uhr	at 1 p.m. / 13:00
gegen	around
gegen sieben Uhr	around 7 a.m.
Mittag	midday
Mitternacht	midnight
eine Sekunde	a second
eine Minute	a minute
eine Stunde	an hour

Colours

die Farbe colour

rot	red	**grau**	grey
blau	blue	**orange**	orange
grün	green	**braun**	brown
gelb	yellow	**rosa**	pink
weiß	white	**lila**	purple
schwarz	black	**silber**	silver

bunt	colourful / bright
hell	light / pale (e.g. **hellgrün** means 'light green')
dunkel	dark (e.g. **dunkelbraun** means 'dark brown')

The Alphabet

A	as in **A**rm	Q	as in **K**uh
B	as in **B**aby	R	as in **E**rd**bee**re
C	as in **Zä**hne	S	as in **ess**en
D	as in **Dä**mon	T	as in **T**ee
E	as in **ze**hn	U	as in **U**-Bahn
F	as in **Eff**ekt	V	as in **fau**lenzen
G	as in **geh**en	W	as in **w**eh
H	as in **H**aar	X	say 'icks'
I	as in **I**gel	Y	say 'üpsilon'
J	as in the English 'yacht'	Z	as in **Zett**el
		ü	say 'ooooow'
K	as in **Kar**l	ä	as in **F**ell
L	as in **el**f	ö	as in the English 'ne**rve**'
M	as in **em**p**fehlen**		
N	as in **En**gel	ß	is a double 's', pronounced 'Eszett'
O	as in o**ben**		
P	as in the English 'pay'		

? Test Yourself

What are the next five words in each sequence?

1. **zwei, vier, sechs...**
2. **Juni, Mai, April...**
3. **Montag, Dienstag...**

Answer this in German:

4. **rot + weiß = ?**

⭐ Stretch Yourself

What is the correct answer in German?

1. **siebzehn x drei = ?**
2. **halb sechs + dreißig Minuten = ?**

Basic German

Being Polite

German has three words for 'you': **du**, **ihr** and **Sie**.

1. You use **du** when speaking to a friend, a family member or an animal. This is an *informal* 'you'. For example:
   Wo wohnst du?
   Where do you live?
2. You use **ihr** when speaking to more than one friend, family member or animal:
   Was macht ihr?
   What are you doing?

3. You use **Sie** when speaking in a *formal* situation, for example, speaking to somebody older than you, a waiter, shopkeeper or stranger:

   Wo wohnen Sie, Herr Fuchs?
   Where do you live, Mr Fox?

   You use **Sie** for both singular and plural, i.e. when you are addressing one person or more than one person.

Greetings and Exclamations

Alles Gute	All the best
Alles Gute zum Geburtstag	Happy birthday
Auf Wiedersehen	Goodbye
Auf Wiederhören	Goodbye (on phone)
Bis bald	See you soon
Bis später / morgen	See you later / tomorrow
Bitte	Please / You're welcome
Danke (schön)	Thank you (very much)
Entschuldigung	Excuse me
Es tut mir Leid	I'm sorry
Gern geschehen	Don't mention it
Grüß Gott	Hello (S. Germany / Austria)
Hallo	Hello
Herzlich willkommen	Welcome
Herzlichen Glückwunsch	Congratulations
Hi	Hi
Ja ≠ Nein	Yes ≠ No
Mit (großem) Vergnügen	With (great) pleasure
Schöne Ferien	Enjoy your holidays
Stimmt	Right
Tschüss	Bye
Entschuldigung / Verzeihung	Pardon me
Viel Glück	Good luck
Wie geht es dir / Ihnen?	How are you?
Wie bitte?	Pardon / What did you say?
Ich verstehe nicht	I don't understand

Question Words

Wann?	When?
Was?	What?
Wer? / Wen? / Wem?	Who? / Whom? / (To) Whom?
Welcher? / Welche? / Welches?	Which?
Wo?	Where?
Warum?	Why?
Wie?	How?
Wie viele?	How many?
Wie lange?	How long?
Was für...?	What kind (of)...?
Mit wem?	With whom / Who with?

Useful Phrases

Auf diese Weise (+ verb)	In this way
Das ist mir egal.	I don't care / mind.
Es kommt darauf an.	It depends.
Es macht nichts.	It doesn't matter.
Es hängt davon ab.	It depends.
gewöhnlich	usually
in Ordnung	OK
Mir geht's gut / schlecht.	I'm fine / unwell.
noch einmal	once again
Schade	shame
Meiner Meinung nach (+ verb)	In my opinion

Connecting Words

Conjunctions are words which join two clauses together and so make your work more complex.

These conjunctions do not affect word order:

aber	but	**oder**	or
denn	as / for	**und**	and
doch	yet	**sondern**	but (rather)

These conjunctions kick the verb to the end of the sentence:

als	when (in the past)
als ob	as if
bevor	before
bis	until
da	since
damit	in order that / so that
dass	that
falls	in case that / if
nachdem	after
ob	whether
obwohl	although
seit	since
sobald	as soon as
während	while / during
weil	because
wenn	if / when

When you use any of the following conjunctions, the verb must come immediately after it:

also	so / therefore
auch	also / to
danach	afterwards
dann	then
dazu	moreover
erstens	first(ly)
natürlich	obviously
so	so
wahrscheinlich	probably
zum Beispiel	for example

Common Abbreviations

Abi	(Abitur) school leaving exam
ADAC	German motorists' organisation
ARD	German television company
BRD	(Bundesrepublik Deutschland) Federal Republic of Germany
DB	(Deutsche Bahn) German railway company
d. h.	i.e.
EU	European Union
gem.	according to
GmbH	Limited company (Ltd)
ICE	Inter-City-Express train
inkl.	included
KFZ	motor vehicle
LKW	lorry
MwSt.	value added tax (VAT)
NRW	Nord-Rhein-Westfalen
PLZ	postcode
usw.	etc.
z. B.	e.g.
ZDF	German television company

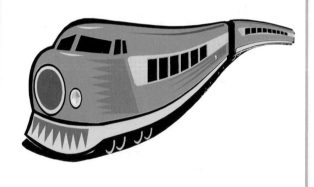

? Test Yourself

How would you say these in German?
1. Why?
2. No
3. Probably
4. See you soon

★ Stretch Yourself

Look at the 'Useful Phrases' section. What phrases are indicated by these initial letters?
1. E m n
2. M M n

◉ Boost Your Memory

Use these five steps to help you learn new words.
1. *Look* at the word carefully.
2. *Say* the word out loud.
3. *Cover* the word with a piece of paper.
4. *Write* the word from memory.
5. *Check* that you have written the word correctly. If not, repeat the steps again.

Personal Information and Family

Talking About Yourself

Ich heiße...	I am called... / My name is...
Ich bin...	I am...
Ich habe...	I have...
Er / Sie heißt...	He / She is called...
Er / Sie ist...	He / She is...
Er / Sie hat...	He / She has...

Mein Vorname ist... und mein Familienname ist...
My first name is... and my surname is...

Ich bin fünfzehn Jahre alt.
I am 15 years old.

Ich habe einen Bruder / eine Schwester.
I have a brother / a sister.

Sie hat zwei Brüder und keine Schwestern.
She has two brothers and no sisters.

Ich bin Einzelkind.
I am an only child.

Meine Schwestern / Meine Brüder heißen...und...
My sisters / My brothers are called...and...

Family Members

die Familie	family	der Enkel / die Enkelin	grandson / granddaughter
die Mutter / Mutti	mother / mum	die Tochter	daughter
der Vater / Vati	father / dad	der Sohn	son
die Eltern	parents	die Stiefmutter	stepmother
die Schwester	sister	der Stiefvater	stepfather
der Bruder	brother	die Halbschwester	half-sister
die Geschwister	brothers and sisters	der Halbbruder	half-brother
die Tante	aunt	die Nichte	niece
der Onkel	uncle	der Neffe	nephew
die Cousine / die Vetterin	cousin (female)	das Mädchen	girl
der Cousin / der Vetter	cousin (male)	der Junge	boy
die Großmutter / Oma	grandmother	der Freund	boyfriend / friend
der Großvater / Opa	grandfather	die Freundin	girlfriend / friend
die Großeltern	grandparents	die Zwillinge	twins

Pets

das Tier / Haustier	animal / pet
der Goldfisch	goldfish
der Hund	dog
das Kaninchen	rabbit
die Maus	mouse
das Meerschweinchen	guinea pig
das Pferd	horse
die Schildkröte	tortoise
das Schaf	sheep
die Schlange	snake (queue)
der Vogel	bird
der Wellensittich	budgerigar

Gender, Singular and Plural

Nouns in German are either masculine (**der**), feminine (**die**) or neuter (**das**). The article in front of the noun tells you what gender the noun is.

- **Der Sohn** and **der Vater** are both masculine, of course, but so are **der Rock** (skirt) and **der Fisch**.
- **Die Oma** and **die Mutter** are both feminine, as you would expect, but so are **die Katze** and **die Maus**.
- **Das Buch** is neuter, but so is **das Mädchen**.

💡 Boost Your Memory

When you learn a new word, you also need to learn its gender. The gender of a word can be found next to the word entry in a dictionary. Here are some tips:

- Most words ending in **–e** and most words ending in **–ung**, **–heit**, **–keit**, **–schaft** and **–nis** are feminine.
- Words ending in **–us** and **–ling** are masculine.
- Words ending in **–chen** and nouns made from infinitives are neuter.

You use **die** for the plural of all genders. There are several ways of forming the plural in German. The plural is usually found in brackets next to the noun in a dictionary. Plurals need to be learned with the noun.

Ending	Example
–e	**Hunde** dogs
–n	**Schwestern** sisters
–en	**Frauen** women
(no ending)	**Monster** monsters
¨	**Brüder** brothers
¨e	**Mäuse** mice
¨er	**Männer** men
–s	**Babys** babies

Build Your Skills: Relative Pronouns

Relative pronouns refer back to a thing or person in a previous sentence and are a great way of linking related sentences. In English they are translated as 'who', 'which' or 'that'. Relative pronouns are mean and kick the verb to the end of the clause.

Ich habe eine Schwester. Sie heißt Laura.

Ich habe eine Schwester, die Laura heißt.
I have a sister, who is called Laura.

Mein Vater heißt Paul. Er hat eine Katze.

Mein Vater, der eine Katze hat, heißt Paul.
My father, who has a cat, is called Paul.

Relative Pronouns

	Masculine	Feminine	Neuter	Plural
Nominative	..., der	..., die	..., das	..., die

My, Your, His and Her

To say 'my' etc. in German you need to know if the word you are describing is masculine, feminine, neuter or plural.
Masculine – **Mein Bruder heißt Ian.**
Feminine – **Meine Mutter ist alt.**
Neuter – **Mein Pferd ist braun.**
Plural – **Meine Mäuse heißen Dip und Dop.**

These possessive adjectives follow the same pattern:

dein	your (sing. informal)
sein	his / its
ihr	her
unser	our
euer	your (plural)
Ihr	your (formal)
ihr	their

❓ Test Yourself

What do these mean in English?
1. **Meine Mutter ist dreiundvierzig Jahre alt.**
2. **Ich habe zwei Schwestern und ein Schaf.**

How do you say these in German?
3. My brother is called John.
4. My mum is an only child but she has a cat.

⭐ Stretch Yourself

1. Say or write in English: '**Ich habe eine Maus, die Ian heißt.**'
2. Say or write in German: 'My stepdad has a son, who is six years old.'

Family and Friends

Describing Appearance

Er / Sie hat...	He / She has...
lange / kurze Haare	long / short hair
lockige / glatte Haare	curly / straight hair
blonde / braune / rote Haare	blond / brown / red hair
keine Haare / eine Glatze	no hair / a bald head
große / kleine / blaue Augen	big / small / blue eyes
einen Bart	a beard
einen Schnurrbart	a moustache

Er / Sie ist...	He / She is...
groß ≠ klein	big ≠ small
dick ≠ schlank	fat ≠ slim
hässlich ≠ schön	ugly ≠ beautiful
jung ≠ alt	young ≠ old
stark ≠ schwach	strong ≠ weak
faul ≠ sportlich	lazy ≠ athletic / sporty
reich ≠ arm	rich ≠ poor

Du hast grüne Augen.
You have green eyes.

Meine Eltern sind schlank und haben braune Haare.
My parents are slim and have brown hair.

Mein Freund ist jung, aber er hat einen Schnurrbart.
My friend is young but he has a moustache.

Er / Sie trägt eine Brille.
He / She wears glasses.

Intensifiers

Make your speaking and writing more interesting by adding intensifiers:

total	totally
sehr	very
wirklich / echt	really
(nicht) zu	(not) too
ziemlich	rather
ganz	quite

Meine Freundin ist sehr hübsch.
My girlfriend is very pretty.

Two Key Verbs – 'Haben' and 'Sein'

The verbs **haben** (to have) and **sein** (to be) are *the* two most important verbs in German. They are very useful for describing people. Here is the present tense of each in full. Make sure you know them:

haben	(to have)
ich habe	I have
du hast	you have
er / sie / es hat	he / she / it has
wir haben	we have
ihr habt	you have (inf. pl.)
sie haben	they have
Sie haben	you have (formal)

sein	(to be)
ich bin	I am
du bist	you are
er / sie / es ist	he / she / it is
wir sind	we are
ihr seid	you are (inf. pl.)
sie sind	they are
Sie sind	you are (formal)

ⓘ Boost Your Memory

Creating a mind map is a good way to learn groups of connected vocabulary. Use lots of colours and images to strengthen the connection in your memory.

The Comparative

To make comparisons add **–er** to the adjective:

klein small ➡ **klein**er smaller
dick fat ➡ **dick**er fatter
schön beautiful ➡ **schön**er more beautiful

Note the irregular forms:

gut good ➡ **besser** better
hoch high ➡ **höher** higher

Some adjectives of one syllable add an umlaut to their vowel:

jung young ➡ **jünger** younger
alt old ➡ **älter** older
groß big ➡ **größer** bigger

Use **als** (than) to compare two things:

Meine Schwester ist jünger als ich.
My sister is younger than me.

Ich bin intelligenter als mein Hund.
I am more intelligent than my dog.

> **✓ Maximise Your Marks**
>
> Make your descriptions more interesting by using **sowohl... als auch...** instead of just listing adjectives, and compare and contrast using **aber**, etc. to gain higher marks.
>
> - **Mein Onkel ist <u>sowohl</u> freundlich <u>als auch</u> fair, <u>aber</u> er ist auch streng.**
>   My uncle is <u>both</u> friendly <u>and</u> fair, <u>but</u> he is also strict.

The Superlative

To say something is 'the most...', add **–ste** to the adjective:

der / die / das kleinste   the smallest
der / die / das dickste   the fattest
der / die / das schönste   the most beautiful

Note the irregular forms:

der / die / das beste   the best
der / die / das höchste   the highest
der / die / das größte   the biggest

Meine Mutter ist auch meine beste Freundin.
My mother is also my best friend.

Emma ist das hübscheste Mädchen auf der ganzen weiten Welt.
Emma is the prettiest girl in the whole wide world.

> **✓ Maximise Your Marks**
>
> Both the comparative and superlative forms take adjective endings when they are describing a noun. See page 28.
> - **Katie und Maeve sind die ältesten Schwestern.**
>   Katie and Maeve are the oldest sisters.
> - **Ich bin das jüngste, aber lustigste Enkelkind.**
>   I am the youngest but funniest grandchild.

❓ Test Yourself

What do these mean in English?
1. **Meine Katze hat große grüne Augen.**
2. **Matthew ist mein bester Freund.**

How do you say these in German?
3. My mother has really curly hair.
4. I am sportier than my brother.

⭐ Stretch Yourself

1. Say or write in English: '**Sie ist jünger als ich und älter als meine Schwester, die ganz faul ist.**'
2. Say or write in German: 'My uncle, who is called Andrew, has the biggest moustache.'

Relationship and Personality

Describing Personality

Positive

Wie kommst du mit deinem Vater aus?
How do you get on with your father?

Ich komme sehr gut mit ihm aus.
I get on very well with him.

Ich verstehe mich auch gut mit meinem Bruder.
I also get on well with my brother.

Wir streiten nie.
We never argue.

Er ist...		He is...
geduldig		patient
freundlich		friendly
gut gelaunt		good-tempered / in a good mood
humorvoll		humorous / amusing
großartig / klasse		great
höflich		polite
frech		cheeky
lustig		funny
hilfsbereit		helpful
fleißig		hard-working
glücklich		happy
verantwortlich		responsible
ordentlich		tidy

Negative

Wie kommst du mit deiner Mutter aus?
How do you get on with your mother?

Ich komme nicht gut mit ihr aus.
I don't get on well with her.

Ich verstehe mich nicht gut mit meiner Schwester.
I don't get on well with my sister.

Wir streiten über alles.
We argue about everything.

Sie ist...		She is...
ungeduldig		impatient
unfreundlich		unfriendly
schlecht gelaunt		bad-tempered / in a bad mood
humorlos		humourless
gemein		mean
unhöflich		impolite
streng		strict
launisch		moody
egoistisch		selfish

Ich kann ihn / sie nicht leiden.
I can't stand him / her.

Er / Sie geht mir auf die Nerven.
He / She gets on my nerves.

Build Your Skills: Combining Adjectives

It is important that you know and include a range of different adjectives in your speaking and written work. However, try to avoid long lists. Use the following expressions to make your work more interesting:
nicht nur..., sondern auch... not only... but also...
sowohl... als auch... both... and / as well as...

Ian ist nicht nur launisch, sondern auch sehr streng.
Ian is not only moody, but also very strict.

Meine Oma ist sowohl geduldig als auch gut gelaunt.
My granny is both patient and good-tempered.

Coordinating Conjunctions

Linking your sentences to make longer sentences enables you to access higher marks for *range of language* in writing and speaking. Here are some easy-to-use linking words that *do not* change the order of a sentence. See page 9 for more conjunctions:

und	and	**oder**	or
aber	but	**denn**	as / for

Meine Tante ist echt lustig, aber mein Onkel ist gemein.
My aunt is really funny, but my uncle is mean.

Your Ideal Partner

Was macht Jungen / Mädchen / dich an?
What attracts boys / girls / you?

Was mich anmacht ist / sind...	What attracts me is / are...
lange Haare	long hair
viel Humor	lots of humour
ein sympathisches Lächeln	a nice smile
ein gepflegtes Aussehen	a well-groomed appearance
eine schöne Figur	a nice figure
geheimnisvolle Augen	mysterious eyes
Komplimente machen	making compliments

Mein idealer Partner / Meine ideale Partnerin ist...	My ideal partner is...
liebevoll	loving
lustig	funny
muskulös	muscular
reich	rich
ruhig	quiet / calm
nachdenklich	thoughtful

Giving Opinions

It is essential that you learn to give opinions in all your work. By developing your sentences this way you will gain extra marks from the examiner. Give a range of points of view, with justifications (reasons why) to back up your ideas, for the highest marks. For example:

Ich liebe...	I love...
Er / Sie liebt...	He / She loves...
Ich hasse...	I hate...
Er / Sie hasst...	He / She hates...
Ich mag...	I like...
Er / Sie mag....	He / She likes...
Ich mag...nicht.	I don't like...
Er / Sie mag...nicht.	He / She doesn't like...
Ich bevorzuge...	I prefer...
Er / Sie bevorzugt...	He / She prefers...
Ich finde ihn / sie...	I find him / her...
Er / Sie findet ihn / sie...	He / She finds him / her...

Relationship Problems

Ich habe ein großes Problem.
I have a big problem.

Ich habe zwei Freundinnen.
I have two girlfriends.

Ich habe viele große Pickel.
I have loads of big spots.

Meine Eltern haben sich getrennt / sind geschieden.
My parents have separated / are divorced.

Ich mag einen Jungen, aber er mag meine beste Freundin.
I like a guy, but he likes my best friend.

✓ Maximise Your Marks

To reach an A or A*, learn some sophisticated phrases to express when someone is unhappy:

- **Meine Eltern waren von meinem Freund überhaupt nicht begeistert.**
  My parents were not at all enthusiastic about my boyfriend.
- **Mein Vater wird sofort wütend, wenn ich über meine Freundin rede.**
  My father gets angry at once, when I talk about my girlfriend.
- **Sie ist von meiner Schwester nicht richtig überzeugt.**
  She is not really convinced about my sister.

? Test Yourself

What do these mean in English?
1. **Mein Bruder geht mir auf die Nerven.**
2. **Ich liebe meine Oma, aber sie ist zu streng.**

How do you say these in German?
3. I can't stand my sister.
4. My ideal partner is rich and muscular.

★ Stretch Yourself

1. Say or write in English: '**Meine Ideale Partnerin ist nicht nur schlank, sondern auch ziemlich liebevoll. Aber ich habe ein großes Problem: Ich habe viele große Pickel und ich mag Pickel nicht.**'
2. Say or write in German: 'My half-brother is both very selfish and bad-tempered, but I love him.'

Future Plans

The Future Tense

To get a grade C or above, it is crucial that you can recognise and use *a range* of tenses. You need to be able to describe things that happened in the past, things that happen now and things that will happen in the future.

The future tense is used to describe a definite plan: something that you *will* do in the future, and is formed as follows:

> **werden** + <u>infinitive</u> of main verb (which goes to the end of the sentence) = future tense

For example:
- **Ich werde neue Schuhe <u>kaufen</u>.**
  I will <u>buy</u> new shoes.

Werden is an important verb and it is also irregular, so you really need to learn it.

ich werde	I will
du wirst	you will
er / sie / es wird	he / she / it will
wir werden	we will
ihr werdet	you will
sie werden	they will
Sie werden	you will

(See page 87 for more on the future tense.)

Useful Verbs

heiraten	to marry
studieren	to study
gehen	to go
feiern	to celebrate
sich verloben	to get engaged
sich verheiraten mit	to get married to
sich freuen auf	to look forward to
werden	to become
reisen	to travel
besuchen	to visit
arbeiten	to work

Build Your Skills: Discussing Aspirations

You can also use the subjunctive form of **mögen** (**möchten**), 'to like', to talk about what you *would like* to do in the future. This would count as another tense in your work and is 'complex language', which gains you higher marks in speaking and writing activities.

This grammatical structure is formed in exactly the same way as the future tense:

> **möchten** + <u>infinitive</u> of main verb (which goes to the end of the sentence)

For example:
- **Ich möchte auf die Universität <u>gehen</u>.**
  I would like <u>to go</u> to university.

Learn how to use **möchten** and show off to the examiner.

ich möchte	I would like
du möchtest	you would like
er / sie / es möchte	he / she / it would like
wir möchten	we would like
ihr möchtet	you would like
sie möchten	they would like
Sie möchten	you would like

Combine the future tense and **möchten** with opinions and justifications when describing events in the future for an amazing impact.

✓ Maximise Your Marks

Aim even higher and also include expressions which need to have the extra word **zu** (+ <u>infinitive</u>) in the sentence. Here are some examples:

hoffen to hope
- **Ich hoffe, in der Zukunft viel Geld <u>zu</u> <u>verdienen</u>.**
  I hope <u>to earn</u> lots of money in the future.

*vorhaben to intend
- **Wir haben vor, nächstes Jahr <u>zu</u> <u>heiraten</u>.**
  We intend <u>to marry</u> next year.

Lust haben to fancy
- **Ich habe Lust, in Deutschland <u>zu</u> <u>studieren</u>.**
  I fancy <u>studying</u> in Germany.

Do not forget to include the comma separating the two clauses.

* Note that **vorhaben** is a separable verb. See page 20.

Discussing Future Plans

das Baby	baby
die Kinder	children
schwanger sein	to be pregnant
der Rentner	pensioner
berühmt werden	to become famous
gratulieren	to congratulate
die Ehe	marriage
der Trauring	wedding ring
die Hochzeit	wedding
verlobt	engaged
die Verlobung	engagement
das Jubiläum	anniversary
die Karriere	career
der / die Millionär / in	millionaire
die Universität	university
die Hochschule	college
die Oberstufe	sixth form

Ich möchte eine erfolgreiche Karriere machen.
I would like to carve out a successful career.

Die Zwillinge werden die Welt beherrschen.
The twins will rule the world.

Ich hoffe, zwei Kinder zu haben.
I hope to have two children.

Katie wird reich und berühmt werden.
Katie will become rich and famous.

Wir möchten eine große Familie und ein Schaf haben.
We would like to have a large family and a sheep.

Möchtest du in Deutschland arbeiten?
Would you like to work in Germany?

Wenn ich Rentner bin, möchte ich Jura studieren.
When I am a pensioner, I would like to study law.

Discussing Marriage

Use the verb **wollen** to discuss what you *want* to do. This is formed the same way as the future tense.

> **wollen** + <u>infinitive</u> of main verb (which goes to the end of the sentence)

For example:
- **Ich will nicht heiraten.**
  I don't want <u>to marry</u>.

(**ich will** means 'I want' in English. Do not get confused!)

wollen	to want (needs to be learned)
ich will	I want
du willst	you want
er / sie / es will	he / she / it wants
wir wollen	we want
ihr wollt	you want
sie wollen	they want
Sie wollen	you want

Ich will heiraten, weil es besser für die Kinder ist.
I want to marry, because it is better for the children.

Ich will heiraten, obwohl ich zuerst die Welt sehen will.
I want to marry, although I want to see the world first.

Ich will nicht heiraten, weil ich reisen will.
I don't want to marry, because I want to travel.

Ich will nicht heiraten, weil meine Eltern geschieden sind.
I don't want to marry, because my parents are divorced.

? Test Yourself

What do these mean in English?
1. **Ich möchte Millionär werden.**
2. **Wir wollen das Jubiläum nicht feiern.**

How do you say these in German?
3. I would like to have 10 children.
4. My brother will study in Berlin.

★ Stretch Yourself

1. Say or write in English: '**Ich habe vor, Deutsch in der Oberstufe zu studieren, aber meine Schwester möchte sowohl heiraten als auch elf Kinder haben!**'
2. Say or write in German: 'My parents hope to become rich and famous, but I just want to go to university.'

House and Home

Describing Where You Live

Wo wohnst du?	Where do you live?

Ich wohne...	I live...
in einem Reihenhaus	in a terraced house
in einem Einfamilienhaus	in a detached house
in einem Doppelhaus	in a semi-detached house
in einem Mehrfamilienhaus	in a block of flats
in einer Wohnung	in a flat
im Erdgeschoss	on the ground floor
im dritten Stock	on the third floor
in der Londonstraße 4	at 4 London Street

Wo liegt das Haus / die Wohnung?
Where is the house / the flat?

Das Haus liegt...	The house is...
Die Wohnung liegt...	The flat is...
am Stadtrand	on the edge of town
in der Stadtmitte	in the town centre
in der Nähe des Stadtzentrums	near the centre of town
auf dem Land	in the countryside
an der Küste	on the coast

The Present Tense – Regular Verbs

The present tense is used to talk about things that you *usually do* or *are doing now*. The present tense in German is equivalent to 'I play' and 'I am playing' in English. Regular verbs all have the same pattern of endings. Here are the three steps to forming the present tense:

1. Take an infinitive, for example: **wohnen** (to live).
2. Take a chainsaw and chop off the **–en**. You are now left with the stem:

   wohn –en

3. Add the following endings to the stem:

ich wohne	I live
du wohnst	you live
er / sie / es wohnt	he / she / it lives
wir wohnen	we live
ihr wohnt	you live
sie wohnen	they live
Sie wohnen	you live

Build Your Skills: Irregular Verbs

Some common verbs do not follow the same regular pattern. There is a change in the stem for the **du** and the **er / sie / es** forms, usually the first vowel. The endings remain the same. For example:

geben	to give
ich gebe	I give
du gibst	you give
er / sie / es gibt	he / she / it gives

fahren	to travel / go
ich fahre	I travel / go
du fährst	you travel / go
er / sie / es fährt	he / she / it travels / goes

A list of irregular verbs can be found on pages 84–85.

💡 Boost Your Memory

Remember verb endings by creating a memorable story using each ending as the beginning of a word. For example:

elephants

standing on

tiptoes

end

to

end

enjoying themselves

My Home

Das Haus hat...	The house has...
ein / zwei Schlafzimmer	one / two bedroom(s)
ein Wohnzimmer	one living room
ein Arbeitszimmer	one study
ein Badezimmer	one bathroom
ein Esszimmer	one dining room

Es gibt...	There is...
einen Garten	a garden
einen Keller	a cellar
einen Flur	a hall
einen Aufzug	a lift
einen Balkon	a balcony
einen Fernseher	a television
einen Sessel	an armchair
einen Tisch	a table
einen Schrank	a wardrobe
einen Teppich	a carpet
eine Küche	a kitchen
eine Toilette	a toilet
eine Dusche	a shower
eine Essecke	a dining area (lit. an eating corner)
eine Kommode	a chest of drawers
ein Bett	a bed

Im Schlafzimmer gibt es einen Fernseher auf dem Tisch.
In the bedroom there is a television on the table.

Im Erdgeschoss gibt es einen Flur und eine Küche neben dem Wohnzimmer.
On the ground floor there is a hall and a kitchen next to the living room.

Es gibt eine Toilette im Schlafzimmer meiner Eltern.
There is a toilet in my parents' bedroom (lit. in the bedroom of my parents).

Wir wohnen in einem Reihenhaus am Stadtrand.
We live in a terraced house on the edge of town.

Mein Schlafzimmer ist total cool, weil es einen Balkon gibt.
My bedroom is totally cool, because there is a balcony.

💡 Boost Your Memory

Es gibt... in German means 'There is...' *or* 'There are...' in English. Use it when listing what you have in your house.

Build Your Skills: Cases

The German language has four cases which define which word for the article ('the' and 'a' etc.) is used. For an A* grade you are expected to use the correct article after each case.

	Masc.	Fem.	Neuter	Plural
Nominative	der	die	das	die
Accusative	den	die	das	die
Genitive	des	der	des	der
Dative	dem	der	dem	den

	Masc.	Fem.	Neuter	Plural*
Nominative	ein	eine	ein	meine
Accusative	einen	eine	ein	meine
Genitive	eines	einer	eines	meiner
Dative	einem	einer	einem	meinen

*possessive adjectives

The *nominative case* is used for the *subject* of the sentence (the thing doing the action).

- Der Mann **hat einen Balkon.**

The *accusative case* is used for the *direct object* (the thing being 'verbed').

- **Der Mann hat** einen Balkon.

The *dative case* is used for the *indirect object* of the sentence (the receiver of the direct object).

- **Khatija gibt** dem Mann **einen Schrank.**

The *genitive case* signifies possession and roughly means 'of the'.

- **Das Schlafzimmer** meiner **Schwester.**
  The bedroom of my sister. / My sister's bedroom.

❓ Test Yourself

What do these mean in English?
1. **Das Haus hat eine Küche und zwei Wohnzimmer.**
2. **Ich wohne in einem Haus auf dem Land.**

How do you say these in German?
3. I live in a flat on the second floor.
4. The house is on the coast.

⭐ Stretch Yourself

1. Learn the present tense endings and then conjugate the present tense of **essen**.
2. What is the direct object of this sentence: '**Das Esszimmer hat einen Tisch**'?

Daily Routine

Reflexive Verbs

Some verbs in German are reflexive. When the person (the subject) doing the action is doing it to themselves, a reflexive verb is used. An example is **sich waschen** (to wash oneself).

A reflexive verb works in the same way as any other verb in the present tense (see page 18) but it also needs a reflexive pronoun to make the verb complete.

Here are the accusative reflexive pronouns:

mich	myself	→	**ich wasche** mich	I wash (myself)
dich	yourself (inf. sing.)	→	**du duschst** dich	you shower (yourself)
sich	himself / herself / itself	→	**sie schminkt** sich	she puts make-up on (herself)
uns	ourselves	→	**wir amüsieren** uns	we enjoy ourselves
euch	yourselves (plural)	→	**ihr rasiert** euch	you shave (yourselves)
sich	themselves	→	**sie benehmen** sich	they behave (themselves)
sich	yourself / yourselves (formal)	→	**Sie streiten** sich	you argue (yourself / yourselves)

The following verbs are reflexive:

sich waschen	to wash	**sich amüsieren**	to enjoy oneself
sich duschen	to shower	**sich benehmen**	to behave
sich rasieren	to shave	**sich streiten**	to argue
sich schminken	to put on make-up	**sich verstehen**	to get on with
		sich ärgern über	to get angry with

> ### 💡 Boost Your Memory
>
> Remember pronouns by turning them into a rap:
>
> **ich, mich, mir**
> **du, dich, dir**
> **sie, sich, sich**
>
> etc.

Build Your Skills: Reflexive Verbs and the Dative

These verbs work in the same way as other reflexive verbs but they have a *dative* reflexive pronoun (different in the **ich** and **du** forms). Using reflexive verbs and the dative correctly is evidence of a Grade A and higher.

Here are the dative reflexive pronouns:

mir	to me
dir	to you
sich	himself / herself / itself
uns	ourselves
euch	yourselves (plural)
sich	themselves
sich	yourself / yourselves

Ich kämme mir die Haare.
I comb my hair.

Ich putze mir die Zähne.
I brush my teeth.

Separable Verbs

Some verbs in German are separable. These verbs work in the same way as any other verb except that they have two parts: the main verb and the prefix. When they are used in a present tense sentence, the prefix jumps to the end. For example:

aufwachen to wake up

Ich wache um sechs Uhr auf.
I wake up at six o'clock.

den Tisch **ab**räumen	to clear the table
aufräumen	to tidy up
aufstehen	to get up
einkaufen	to shop
den Müll **raus**bringen	to take out the rubbish
staubsaugen	to vacuum
staubwischen	to dust
vorbereiten	to prepare
weitermachen	to continue
sich **an**ziehen	to get dressed

Separable Verbs (cont.)

Attention! There are some verbs with prefixes that look separable but are not: verbs starting with **be–**, **emp–**, **ent–**, **ge–**, **ver–** and **zer–** are *in*separable.

Build Your Skills: Time, Frequency and Word Order

Frequency words like **oft**, **manchmal** and **jeden Tag** and time words like **jetzt**, **abends**, **gestern** and **morgen** add depth to your work. These words are usually placed straight after the verb in German. Notice the verb is the second idea:

1	2	3	
Ich	sauge	<u>jeden Tag</u>	staub.
I vacuum <u>every day</u>.			

But often they can start a sentence. When a time word is at the beginning of a sentence, the verb and subject need to swap places, so that the verb stays the second idea. Notice how the **sauge** and **ich** change places:

1	2	3	
<u>Jeden Tag</u>	sauge	ich	staub.
<u>Every day</u> I vacuum.			

This is known as inversion and is a great way of gaining higher marks in your writing and speaking.

See page 32 for more time words and frequency words.

Discussing Daily Routine

Was machst du, um deinen Eltern zu helfen?
What do you do to help your parents?

Ich mähe ab und zu den Rasen.
I mow the lawn now and again.

Ich muss jede Woche mein Zimmer aufräumen.
I have to tidy my room every week.

Ich muss im Haushalt helfen, um Geld zu verdienen.
I have to help around the house to earn money.

Ich räume nie auf, weil ich keine Zeit habe.
I never tidy up, because I don't have time.

Wenn ich Kinder habe, werden sie…	If I have children, they will…
die Wäsche in die Waschmaschine tun	put the washing in the washing machine
das Bett machen	make the bed
das Frühstück vorbereiten	prepare breakfast

Wann beginnt ein typischer Tag für Sie?
When does a typical day for you begin?

Um fünf Uhr stehe ich auf.
At five o'clock I wake up.

Dann rasiere ich mich.
Then I shave.

Normalerweise ziehe ich mich schnell an.
Usually I get dressed quickly.

❓ Test Yourself

1. What are the seven accusative reflexive pronouns?
2. What is special about a separable verb?
3. **Was machst du, um deinen Eltern zu helfen?** (List three things in German.)

⭐ Stretch Yourself

1. Say or write in English: '**Normalerweise stehe ich früh auf, aber morgen werde ich um neun Uhr aufstehen.**'
2. Say or write in German: 'Every day you comb your hair.'

Local Environment

Your Local Area

Here are some useful questions and answers when discussing your home town.

Wo wohnst du?   Where do you live?
Ich wohne in Crewe.   I live in Crewe.
Wo liegt Crewe?   Where is Crewe?

Crewe liegt im Nordwesten von England.
Crewe is in the north west of England.

im Norden   in the north
im Süden   in the south
im Osten   in the east
im Westen   in the west

ungefähr dreißig Kilometer von Manchester entfernt
about 30 kilometres away from Manchester

Die Stadt hat...	The town has...
ungefähr...Einwohner	about...inhabitants
viel zu bieten	a lot to offer

Hier gibt es...	There is...here.
(k)einen Skatepark	(not) a skatepark
(k)einen Flughafen	(not) an airport
(k)einen Jugendklub	(not) a youth club
(k)eine Fußgängerzone	(not) a pedestrian zone
(k)ein Sportzentrum	(not) a sports centre
(k)ein Hallenbad	(not) a swimming pool
(k)ein Schloss	(not) a castle

Build Your Skills: Using 'Man Kann...'

Man in German means 'one' or a general 'you' in English. It is impersonal and adds more variety to your language. For higher marks in your work the examiner wants to see other subjects in your work, apart from just **ich** all of the time.

Man kann... (+ infinitive)   You can (+ infinitive)...

Man kann schwimmen gehen.
You can go swimming.

Was kann man in deiner Gegend machen?
What can you do in your neighbourhood?

Man kann...	You can...
Hier kann man...	Here you can...
angeln gehen	go fishing
einkaufen gehen	go shopping
ein Museum besuchen	visit a museum
Segelkurse machen	do sailing courses
am Strand spielen	play on the beach

✔ Maximise Your Marks

Notice that **man** has only *one* **n** and should not be confused with **der Mann** (the man). Accuracy in your writing is important for higher grades.

Saying What You Prefer

Giving and understanding opinions is a very important part of your exam. The more you give and justify, the higher your mark. Using a range of opinion phrases is also important.

Here are some useful expressions to indicate preference:

gern (with pleasure – i.e. like doing something)
- **Ich gehe gern ins Sportzentrum.**
  I like going to the sports centre.

nicht gern (with no pleasure – i.e. dislike doing something)
- **Ich wohne nicht gern auf dem Land.**
  I don't like living in the countryside.

lieber (prefer doing something)
- **Wir hängen lieber im Park rum.**
  We prefer hanging around in the park.

am liebsten (best of all)
- **Die Jugendlichen gehen am liebsten ins Kino.**
  Young people like going to the cinema best of all.

Build Your Skills: Subordinating Conjunctions

You need to use a wide range of subordinating conjunctions for a Grade A and above. As well as , **weil** and , **wenn**, you can also use , **wo** (where) when describing your home town. For example:

Das ist die alte Wohnung, wo **wir gewohnt haben.**
That is the old flat where we lived.

In der Gegend gibt es einen großen Fischmarkt, wo **man viele Fischsorten kaufen kann.**
In the area there is a large fish market where you can buy lots of different kinds of fish.

Discussing Where You Live

Die Gegend ist...	The area is...
grün	green
wunderbar	wonderful
sicher	safe
gefährlich	dangerous
deprimierend	depressing
sauber	clean
modern	modern
freundlich	friendly
todlangweilig	deadly boring
lebendig	lively
ruhig	peaceful
leise	quiet

Die Landschaft um...ist ziemlich schön.
The landscape around...is quite beautiful.

Wo wirst du in der Zukunft wohnen?
Where will you live in the future?

In der Zukunft werde ich...wohnen.
In the future I will live...

in einer Wohnung am Meer / Fluss
in a flat by the sea / river

Es wird...geben.	There will be...
keine / viele **Graffiti**	no / lots of graffiti
keine / viele **Radwege**	no / lots of cycle paths
keine / viele **Geschäfte**	no / lots of shops
keinen / viel **Lärm**	no / lots of noise
keinen / viel **Verkehr**	no / lots of traffic

Ich wünsche mir auch...ganz in der Nähe.
I would also like...close by.

ein**en** Freizeitpark	an amusement park
ein**en** Obstmarkt	a fruit market
ein**e** Disko	a disco
ein gutes Lokal	a good pub

Build Your Skills: Great Expressions

Use some of these expressions in your work to impress the examiner and gain higher marks:

Im Großen und Ganzen (verb)**...**
On the whole...

Ein großer Vorteil ist...
A big advantage is...

Der größte Nachteil ist, dass... (verb)
The biggest disadvantage is that...

Das Gute daran ist, dass... (verb)
The good thing about it is that...

Take care with word order:

Im Großen und Ganzen spiele ich lieber am Strand.
On the whole I prefer playing on the beach.

Ein großer Vorteil ist der coole Skatepark.
A big advantage is the cool skate park.

❓ Test Yourself

What does this mean in English?
1. **Ich besuche Museen nicht gern, weil sie deprimierend sind.**

How do you say these in German?
2. The town has around 70,000 inhabitants and a lot to offer.
3. The area is clean but there is a lot of noise.

⭐ Stretch Yourself

1. Say or write in English: '**Abends gibt es eine Disko, wo man rumhängen kann, obwohl der größte Vorteil ist, dass es auch einen tollen Freizeitpark gibt.**'
2. Say or write in German: 'On the whole the town is quite lively.'

Practice Questions

 Complete these exam-style questions to test your skills and understanding. Check your answers on page 90. You may wish to answer these questions on a separate piece of paper.

Reading

1 Fill the gaps in the following passage using six of the seven words below:

möchten   hat   heißt   Schnurrbart   Familienname   werde   Eltern

> Guten Tag! Mein Vorname ist Jens und mein (a) .... (1) ist Schmidt. Ich bin fünfzehn
>
> Jahre alt und komme aus Hamburg. Ich habe einen Bruder, der Igor (b) .... , (1) und
>
> eine Schwester, die eine Katze (c) .... (1). Ich komme sehr gut mit meinen
>
> (d) .... (1) aus, obwohl mein Vater, der einen (e) .... (1) hat, ab und
>
> zu schlecht gelaunt ist. Meine Eltern haben früh geheiratet, aber ich (f) .... (1) nicht
>
> heiraten, weil ich eine erfolgreiche Karriere machen möchte.

2 Read the text below and answer the questions in English.

> Herr Opp schreibt über seine Stadt:
>
> Ich wohne zur Zeit in Mannheim. Sie liegt in Südwestdeutschland ungefähr siebzig Kilometer von Frankfurt am Main entfernt. Es ist eine große Industriestadt am Fluss. Im Stadtzentrum gibt es ein schönes, altes Schloss, eine Universität, ein modernes Theater und viele Geschäfte. Es gibt viel zu sehen, aber ich wohne nicht gern hier, weil es ziemlich langweilig ist und, weil man nicht segeln gehen kann.'
>
> Früher habe ich am Meer in Norddeutschland gewohnt. Das war total ruhig und sauber, nicht wie hier! Ich habe gern dort gewohnt. In der Zukunft möchte ich in der Schweiz wohnen, wo es ganz grün und sicher ist, weil man dort jeden Tag reiten und angeln gehen kann. Ich liebe Tiere! Ich möchte eine große Wohnung mit zehn Balkonen kaufen und viele Kinder haben. Der größte Vorteil des Landlebens ist, dass es keinen Verkehr oder Lärm gibt.

a) Where does Herr Opp live?

.... (3)

b) What can you visit there?

.... (4)

c) Does he like living there? Why? Why not?

.... (3)

d) Where did he used to live?

.... (1)

e) Where would he like to live and why?

.... (5)

f) What is the biggest advantage of this lifestyle?

.... (2)

Speaking

3 You are going to be interviewed about your life in the UK by a German radio station. Prepare to answer in full sentences, giving opinions and developing your answers where possible. When you are ready, record yourself on your mobile phone.

    a) Talk about yourself – name, age, family, etc.

    b) Describe your appearance.

    c) What kind of person are you?

    d) Do you get on well with your parents? Why (not)?

    e) Describe your town and where you will live in the future.

    (10)

Writing

4 You have been tasked with creating a new cartoon character for a German magazine. You need to write about each of the following aspects of your character for the magazine's editors. Give opinions too.

- The character's name, appearance and personality
- The character's family life and relationships with others
- A description of the house and town where your character lives

(15)

5 You have been asked to write about your future plans. Discuss and give opinions on the following.

- Will you marry? Have children? Why? Why not?
- Where will you live in the future and what will it be like and why?
- What would you like to do when you are a pensioner and why?

(15)

How well did you do?

| 0–16 | Try again | 17–32 | Getting there | 33–49 | Good work | 50–64 | Excellent! |

School and School Subjects

School Subjects

It is important that you can say the subjects that you study and that you can understand the others.

Was ist dein Lieblingsfach?
What is your favourite subject?

Mein Lieblingsfach ist...	My favourite subject is...
Meine Lieblingsfächer sind...	My favourite subjects are...

(die) **Biologie**	biology
(die) **Chemie**	chemistry
(das) **Deutsch**	German
(das) **Englisch**	English
(die) **Erdkunde**	geography
(das) **Französisch**	French
(die) **Fremdsprachen**	foreign languages
(die) **Geografie**	geography
(die) **Geschichte**	history
(die) **Informatik**	ICT
(das) **Kochen**	cooking
(die) **Kunst**	art
(das) **Latein**	Latin
(die) **Mathe(matik)**	maths
(die) **Musik**	music
(die) **Naturwissenschaften**	science
(die) **Physik**	physics
(die) **Religion**	RE
(die) **Sozialkunde**	sociology
(das) **Spanisch**	Spanish
(der) **Sport**	PE / sport
(die) **Technologie**	technology
(das) **Theater**	drama
(das) **Turnen**	PE / gymnastics
(das) **Werken**	design technology

✓ Maximise Your Marks

When talking about your school subjects, you do *not* need to use **der**, **die** or **das**.
For example:
- **Mein Lieblingsfach ist Deutsch**.
  My favourite subject is German.

Describing Subjects and Teachers

It is vital that you get in the habit of giving opinions about everything you say. Do not repeat the same adjective – not everything is **langweilig** (boring). Use a variety of adjectives with intensifiers in front of them to get higher marks – **ziemlich / sehr / nicht so langweilig** etc.

Use these words to give positive opinions:

einfach / leicht	easy
interessant	interesting
locker	relaxed
logisch	logical
lustig	funny
nützlich	useful
praktisch	practical
sympathisch	pleasant

Es macht viel Spaß.
It's lots of fun.

Der Lehrer / Die Lehrerin ist...
The teacher is...

Ich bin sehr gut in...
I am very good at...

Ich finde Politik...
I find politics...

Use these words to give negative opinions:

schwierig / schwer	difficult
langweilig	boring
streng	strict
kompliziert	complicated
furchtbar	awful / terrible
nutzlos	pointless
unmöglich	impossible
mies	rubbish

Es macht keinen Spaß.
It's no fun.

Die Lehrer / Lehrerinnen sind...
The teachers are...

Mathe fällt mir schwer.
I find maths difficult.

Kunst kann ich nicht leiden.
I can't stand art.

Englisch ist schwieriger als Informatik.
English is <u>more</u> difficult <u>than</u> ICT.

Build Your Skills: Giving Reasons Why

I am the Vile Weil Welly. I sound so vile because I kick the closest verb to the end of the sentence. My best friend Comma is *always* one step behind me.

When you want to give reasons why you like or dislike something, use me, because (**weil**) I make your work more complex and so boost up your writing and speaking grades!

I have other subordinating conjunction mates that are just as vile as me, kicking verbs to the end of the sentence:

, dass (that) **, wenn** (, if / when) **, obwohl** (, although) **, während** (, while) **, damit** (, so that / in order that)

Look what I can do:

Mein Lieblingsfach ist Deutsch. Es ist lustig.
My favourite subject is German. It is funny.

Here I come…

Mein Lieblingsfach ist Deutsch, weil es lustig ist.
My favourite subject is German, because it is funny.

See pages 9 and 45 for more subordinating conjunctions.

💡 Boost Your Memory

Use this rhyme to help you remember that **weil** and other subordinating conjunctions kick the first verb to the end of the sentence.

'The Vile Weil Welly is so vile, he kicks the verbs a country mile (to the end of the sentence)'

Talking About Your School

There is a lot of school-related vocabulary that examiners can use in the reading and listening exams. Look back over the vocabulary your teacher has given you. Here are some useful phrases:

Ich habe Erdkunde montags / dienstags / zweimal in der Woche.
I have geography on Mondays / Tuesdays / twice a week.

Unsere Schule liegt in der Stadtmitte.
Our school is in the town centre.

Die Schule ist größtenteils dreckig / alt / modern.
The school is mostly dirty / old / modern.

Es gibt 1.000 Schüler.
There are 1000 pupils.

Die Klassenzimmer sind...
The classrooms are....

Ich bin in der neunten Klasse.
I am in Year 9.

Wir haben...	We have...
eine Sporthalle	a sportshall
eine Kantine	a canteen
eine Bibliothek	a library
eine Aula	a hall
eine Turnhalle	a gym
eine (Mittags)Pause	a (lunch)break
einen Schulhof	a playground

Nach der Schule gibt es...	After school there is / are...
einen Chor	a choir
ein Orchester	an orchestra
viele / keine AGs	no / lots of clubs

❓ Test Yourself

What does this mean in English?
1. **Chemie kann ich nicht leiden. Sie macht keinen Spaß.**

How do you say these in German?
2. My favourite subjects are history and maths.
3. I find Mr Smith very pleasant and fair.

⭐ Stretch Yourself

1. Say or write in English: '**Meine Schule kann ich nicht leiden, weil die Klassenzimmer sowohl dreckig als auch alt sind.**'

2. Say or write in German: 'My favourite subject is ICT, because the teacher is really relaxed.'

School Rules and School Uniform

School Uniform

Was trägst du in der Schule?
What do you wear at school?

In der Schule muss ich... tragen.	At school I have to wear...
einen Rock	a skirt
einen Pullover	a jumper
einen Blazer	a blazer
einen Schlips	a tie
eine Hose	a pair of trousers
eine Krawatte	a tie
eine Bluse	a blouse
eine Jacke	a jacket
eine Strumpfhose	tights
ein Hemd	a shirt
ein Kleid	a dress
ein Sweatshirt	a sweatshirt
die Schuhe	shoes
die Socken	socks
die Sportschuhe	trainers

Discussing School Uniform

Bist du für oder gegen eine Schuluniform?
Are you for or against a school uniform?

Ich bin total (da)für / (da)gegen.
I am totally for (it) / against (it).

Es gibt mehr Nachteile als Vorteile.
There are more disadvantages than advantages.

Man verliert seine Individualität.
You lose your individuality.

Alle sehen gleich aus.
Everybody looks the same.

Man leidet nicht unter Diskriminierung / Mobbing.
You don't suffer from discrimination / bullying.

Mode gehört nicht in der Schule.
Fashion doesn't belong at school.

Man weiß morgens genau, was man anziehen soll.
You know exactly what you will wear in the mornings.

Ein anderer Vorteil / Nachteil ist, dass...(verb).
Another advantage / disadvantage is that...

Build Your Skills: Adjective Endings

Using a variety of adjectives in your work gains you higher marks. Adjectives must agree with the number, gender and case of the noun. This is done by adding an ending to the adjective.

The first table shows the adjective endings to use after the indefinite article **ein** ('a' or 'an') and **kein** (no), and after **mein** (my), **dein** (your), **sein** (his / its), **ihr** (her), **unser** (our), **euer** (your), **ihr** (their), **Ihr** (your, formal), and **all** (all).

The second table shows the adjective endings to use when there is no article, and after **viel** (many), **etwas** (some), **mehr** (more), **wenig** (few), and **mehrere** (several).

Using the correct adjective ending will increase your accuracy score for speaking and writing.

	Masculine	Feminine	Neuter	Plural
Nom.	ein roter Blazer	eine rote Bluse	ein rotes Hemd	keine roten Sportschuhe
Acc.	einen roten Blazer	eine rote Bluse	ein rotes Hemd	keine roten Sportschuhe
Dat.	einem roten Blazer	einer roten Bluse	einem roten Hemd	keinen roten Sportschuhen

	Masculine	Feminine	Neuter	Plural
Nom.	brauner Dreck	freie Wahl	kaltes Wasser	rote Schuhe
Acc.	braunen Dreck	freie Wahl	kaltes Wasser	rote Schuhe
Dat.	braunem Dreck	freier Wahl	kaltem Wasser	roten Schuhen

- **Wir müssen einen schwarzen Blazer und ein weißes Hemd mit schwarzen Schuhen tragen.**
  We have to wear a black blazer and a white shirt with black shoes.

School and Work

Modal Verbs

Modal verbs are useful verbs which are used with the infinitive of another verb. The infinitive goes at the end of the sentence.

For example:

Man muss eine Uniform <u>tragen</u>.
You have to wear a uniform.

können to be able to / can	müssen to have to	dürfen to be allowed to	sollen to ought to	wollen to want to	mögen to like to
ich kann	ich muss	ich darf	ich soll	ich will	ich mag
du kannst	du musst	du darfst	du sollst	du willst	du magst
man / er kann	man / er muss	man / er darf	man / er soll	man / er will	man / er mag
wir können	wir müssen	wir dürfen	wir sollen	wir wollen	wir mögen
ihr könnt	ihr müsst	ihr dürft	ihr sollt	ihr wollt	ihr mögt
sie können	sie müssen	sie dürfen	sie sollen	sie wollen	sie mögen
Sie können	Sie müssen	Sie dürfen	Sie sollen	Sie wollen	Sie mögen

School Rules and Sentence Structure

Subject	Second	(Time)	(Manner)	(Place)	Final
Man	muss	jeden Tag	pünktlich	zur Schule	kommen.
You have to get to school on time every day.					
Man	darf	nie		in der Schule	rauchen.
You are never allowed to smoke in school.					
Man	soll		keinen Kaugummi	in den Klassenzimmern	kauen.
You shall not chew chewing gum in the classrooms.					

There are strict rules for where words go in German sentences. The first verb always needs to be the second idea. All other verbs are the *final idea* of the sentence. Within a sentence, time words come first, then manner words (how), then place words (location). See above for examples of this.

✓ Maximise Your Marks

Use a variety of complex opinion starters to improve your writing and speaking grades:

Meiner Meinung nach (verb)**...** In my opinion...
- **Meiner Meinung nach ist das total unfair.**
  In my opinion that is totally unfair.

Ich denke, dass... (verb). I think that...
- **Ich denke, dass es eine gute Regel ist.**
  I think that it is a good rule.

Ich bin der Meinung, dass... (verb). I am of the opinion that...
- **Ich bin der Meinung, dass Mathe toll ist.**
  I am of the opinion that maths is great.

? Test Yourself

What does this mean in English?

1 **Man leidet nicht unter Mobbing.**

How do you say these in German?

2 You are not allowed to smoke at school.

3 You have to wear a blazer and a tie at school.

★ Stretch Yourself

1 Say or write in English: '**Ich bin total gegen die Schuluniform. Meiner Meinung nach ist das wirklich unpraktisch.**'

2 Say or write in German: 'You have to wear a blue blazer, a stripy tie and black shoes.'

Pressures at School

Pressures at School

Ich habe Angst vor (+ dative case)...	I am afraid of...
Ich habe Probleme mit (+ dative case)...	I have problems with...

dem Unterricht	the lessons
den Prüfungen	the exams
den Lehrern	the teachers
Messern	knives
Mobbing	bullying
Spinnen	spiders

Ich habe keine Freunde.
I have no friends.

Die Hausaufgaben finde ich stressig.
I find the homework stressful.

Meine Mitschüler mobben mich.
My classmates bully me.

Ich bekomme schlechte Noten.
I get bad grades.

Viele Schüler fühlen sich in der Schule nicht sicher.
Many pupils don't feel safe at school.

Build Your Skills: The Definite Article (The)

There are 16 different ways of saying 'the' in German depending on the gender, number and case of the noun. The case depends on where the noun is in a sentence or which preposition comes before it.

Here we will concentrate on the *dative case*. This case is *always* used after the following prepositions:

aus (from), **außer** (except), **bei** (at), **mit** (with), **nach** (after / to), **seit** (since), **von** (from) and **zu** (to)

And after these prepositions *when there is no movement towards a place*:

an (at), **auf** (on), **hinter** (behind), **in** (in), **unter** (under), **neben** (next to), **zwischen** (between), **vor** (in front of), **über** (over)

For example:

- **Ich habe Angst vor den Prüfungen.**
  I am afraid of the exams.
- **Ich habe Probleme mit dem Englischlehrer.**
  I have problems with the English teacher.

	Masc.	Fem.	Neuter	Plural
Nominative	der	die	das	die
Accusative	den	die	das	die
Genitive	des*	der	des*	der
Dative	dem	der	dem	den**

* Add **–s** or **–es** to the end of the noun.
** Add **–n** to the end of the noun.

In My Dream School

Developing an answer in your writing and speaking will gain you marks for content or communication. Use a variety of tenses in your work for best results.

Wie wird deine Traumschule aussehen?
How will your dream school look?

Es wird zehn Schüler in einer Schulklasse geben.
There will be ten pupils in a class.

Jeder Schüler wird seinen eigenen Computer haben.
Every pupil will have their own computer.

Wir werden keine Hausaufgaben oder Prüfungen haben.
We will have no homework or exams.

Die Schule wird um halb elf beginnen.
School will start at half past ten.

Handys werden erlaubt sein.
Mobile phones will be allowed.

Hier wird man eigene Klamotten tragen können.
You will be able to wear your own clothes here.

Build Your Skills: The Conditional Mood

You use the verb **würden** to say what you *would do* in German, with the infinitive at the end of the sentence.

ich würde	I would
du würdest	you would
er / sie / es würde	he / she / it would
wir würden	we would
ihr würdet	you would
sie würden	they would
Sie würden	you would

Ich würde Jeans in meiner Traumschule tragen.
I would wear jeans in my dream school.

Build Your Skills: 'If I Were You...'

For outstanding effects, combine the conditional mood and the subordinate clause rules explained above, with the imperfect subjunctive. The two main imperfect subjunctive forms seen at GCSE, apart from **möchten** (would like), are those of the verbs **haben** (to have) and **sein** (to be). For example:

Wenn ich Schulleiter wäre, würde ich neue Regeln einführen.
If I <u>were</u> headmaster, I would introduce new rules.

Wenn ich Probleme mit Mobbing hätte, würde ich mit meinem Lehrer sprechen.
If I <u>had</u> problems with bullying, I would speak to my teacher.

Subordinate Clauses

A subordinate clause is introduced by a subordinating conjunction (see page 27), which kicks the first verb to the end of the clause. This is followed directly by a comma and the next verb in the second clause. For example:

<u>Wenn</u> ich zu spät zur Schule <u>komme</u>, <u>muss</u> ich fünfzehn Minuten nachsitzen.
<u>If</u> / <u>when</u> I <u>arrive</u> too late to school, I <u>get</u> 15 minutes detention.

<u>Obwohl</u> ich gut in Mathe <u>bin</u>, <u>habe</u> ich Angst vor den Prüfungen.
<u>Although</u> I <u>am</u> good at maths, I <u>am</u> afraid of the exams.

A subordinate clause does not have to be at the beginning of the sentence. For example:

Ich <u>muss</u> fünfzehn Minuten nachsitzen, <u>wenn</u> ich zu spät zur Schule <u>komme</u>.
I <u>get</u> 15 minutes detention <u>if</u> / <u>when</u> I <u>arrive</u> too late to school.

💡 Boost Your Memory

Remember word order for subordinate clauses starting with words like **wenn** (if / when) by imagining the verbs sharing a first kiss over a comma fence:

- **Wenn ich Millionär wäre, würde ich meine eigene Schule bauen.**
  If I <u>were</u> a millionaire, I <u>would</u> build my own school.

❓ Test Yourself

What does this mean in English?

1. **Obwohl ich Probleme mit dem Unterricht habe, bekomme ich gute Noten.**
2. **Ich habe Angst vor Mathe.**

How do you say these in German?

3. I have problems with exams and the teachers.
4. The school will begin at eleven o'clock.

⭐ Stretch Yourself

1. Say or write in English: '**Wenn ich keine Freunde hätte, würden mich die anderen Mitschüler mobben.**'
2. Say or write in German: 'If I had bad grades, I would have problems with my parents.'

Part-time Work

Part-time Jobs

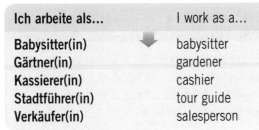

The topic of part-time work is a great subject for you to develop a response.

Hast du einen Teilzeitjob?
Do you have a part-time job?

Ja, ich habe einen Teilzeitjob.
Yes, I have a part-time job.

Nein, ich habe keinen Teilzeitjob.
No, I don't have a part-time job.

Was für einen Teilzeitjob hast du?
What kind of part-time job do you have?

Ich trage Zeitungen aus.
I deliver newspapers.

Ich arbeite als...	I work as a...
Babysitter(in)	babysitter
Gärtner(in)	gardener
Kassierer(in)	cashier
Stadtführer(in)	tour guide
Verkäufer(in)	salesperson

Wo arbeitest du?
Where do you work?

Ich arbeite...	I work...
in einem Supermarkt	in a supermarket
in einem Geschäft	in a shop
in einem Sportgeschäft	in a sports shop
in einer Fabrik	in a factory
an einer Tankstelle	at a petrol station.

Ich arbeite als Kellner in einem Restaurant.
I work as a waiter in a restaurant.

✓ Maximise Your Marks

Distinguishing between male and female jobs in German is easy. Most female jobs end in –**in**. Remember this (especially if you are female!). Here are the common language patterns when describing jobs:

Arzt ≠ Ärztin	doctor ≠ female doctor
Zahnarzt ≠ Zahnärztin	dentist ≠ female dentist
Kellner ≠ Kellnerin	waiter ≠ waitress

Saying When and How Much

It is good practice to add time words and frequency words into your sentences. The examiner is looking for this and any extra details that you can include to make your writing and speaking more interesting. Listening and reading papers will often be full of these words, so it is to your advantage to be able to recognise them.

Wann arbeitest du?
When do you work?

Ich arbeite...	I work...
am Wochenende	at the weekend
am Samstag / Sonnabend	on Saturday
samstags / sonnabends	on Saturdays
jeden Tag (außer Montag)	every day (except Monday)
jeden zweiten Sonntag	every second Sunday
ab und zu	now and then
einmal in der Woche	once a week
zweimal im Monat	twice a month
neun Stunden in der Woche	nine hours a week
morgens	in the morning(s)
abends	in the evening(s)
nach der Schule	after school

Wie viel verdienst du?
How much do you earn?

Ich verdiene... Ich bekomme...	I earn... I get...
7€ pro Stunde	€7 per hour
35€ pro Woche	€35 per week
ganz viel Geld	quite a lot of money

Opinions About Part-time Jobs

Give opinions about everything. There are so many adjectives, so do not just use the same ones; and have a good bank of opinion words ready for all occasions. For higher marks, remember to justify your opinions.

Wie ist dein Teilzeitjob?
How is your part-time job?

Ich finde die Arbeit...	I find the work...
schwer	difficult
gut bezahlt	well paid
schlecht bezahlt	badly paid
anstrengend	exhausting
langweilig	boring
interessant	interesting

Ich bin gern im Freien.	I like being in the open.
Es macht (keinen) Spaß.	It is (no) fun.
Ich arbeite gern allein.	I like working alone.
Es gibt viel zu tun.	There is a lot to do.

Ich mache gern etwas Praktisches.
I like doing practical things.

Pocket Money

Mit meinem Taschengeld / meinem Lohn kaufe ich...	With my pocket money / my wages I buy...
(die) Computerspiele	computer games
(das) Make-up	make-up
(die) Kleider / Klamotten	clothes / clobber
(das) Schulmaterial	things for school
(die) Süßigkeiten	sweets
(das) Guthaben	credit (for a mobile phone)

Ich will Geld sparen,..	I want to save money...
um einen neuen Computer zu kaufen	in order to buy a new computer
um in Urlaub zu gehen	in order to go on holiday

Build Your Skills: Developing Conversations

Add intensifiers, opinions and negatives to your sentences to make them more interesting.

You should also add more complex structures to your work, using words such as **dass**, **obwohl**, **weil** (do not forget the comma before these words, and remember where the verb goes). Use the words in sentences with more than one clause for a great effect:

Ich denke, <u>dass</u> die Arbeit echt anstrengend ist,...
I think <u>that</u> the work is really exhausting,...

<u>obwohl</u> ich den Job mag,...
<u>although</u> I like the job,...

<u>weil</u> ich gern in einem kleinen Team bin,...
<u>because</u> I like being in a small team,...

<u>jedoch</u> möchte **ich mehr Geld verdienen.**
<u>however</u>, I would like to earn more money.

❓ Test Yourself

What does this mean in English?
1. **Ich verdiene 40€ pro Woche. Ich finde die Arbeit gut bezahlt.**
2. **Mit meinem Taschengeld kaufe ich Kleider.**

How do you say these in German?
3. I work as a female sales assistant in a sports shop.
4. I work five hours per week on Saturdays.

⭐ Stretch Yourself

1. Say or write in English: '**Ich denke, dass die Arbeit sehr gut bezahlt ist, obwohl ich den Job hasse, weil man abends arbeiten muss, und ich finde das total anstrengend.**'
2. Say or write in German: 'I work twice a week in a factory. I love the job, because I like working in a team, although my friend earns more than me.'

Jobs and Work Experience

The Perfect Tense

The perfect tense is used to talk about things which *happened* or *have happened* and *were completed* in the past. It is good practice to include as many tenses as possible in your work.

The perfect tense is made up of two parts:

haben or **sein** + past participle

Ich habe ein Praktikum bei BMW gemacht.
I did a work placement at BMW.
or I have done a work placement at BMW.

The Past Participle – Irregular Verbs

The past participles of irregular verbs do not follow the regular pattern. They need to be learnt. Learn as many as you can. You can find some of the main ones on pages 84–85 or at the back or middle of a good dictionary:

Ich habe...gegessen	I ate / have eaten...
Ich habe...verbracht	I spent / have spent...
Ich habe...geschrieben	I wrote / have written...

The Past Participle – Regular Verbs

All regular verbs take **haben** as an auxiliary verb.

Here is how you form the past participle of regular verbs:
1. Take the infinitive: **tippen** (to type), for example.
2. Take a chainsaw and chop off the **–en** to find the stem:
   tipp –en
3. Glue **ge–** to the front and **–t** to the end of the stem (or **–et** if the stem ends in **–t**).

Ich habe Briefe getippt.
I typed / have typed letters.

Ich habe als Friseurin gearbeitet.
I worked / have worked as a hairdresser.

Regular verbs that start with **be–**, **ver–** or **zer–**, or that end in **–ieren**, do not need a **ge–** to be added. For example:
Ich habe die Kunden bedient.
I served / have served the customers.

Ich habe alles fotokopiert.
I photocopied / have photocopied everything.

Build Your Skills: The Perfect Tense – Verbs with 'Sein'

There are some verbs that form the perfect tense using **sein** instead of **haben**. Most of these verbs describe movement from one place to another. These verbs have mostly *irregular* past participles and need to be learnt. You can find these verbs on pages 84–85 (they are marked with *).

sein... + past participle

ich bin...ge**fahr**en	I travelled / have travelled...
du bist...ge**gang**en	you went / have gone...
er ist...ge**komm**en	he came / has come...
wir sind...ge**fall**en	we fell / have fallen
ihr seid...gewesen	you were / have been...
sie sind...gestiegen	they climbed / have climbed...
Sie sind...geworden	you became / have become...

Work Experience

Wo hast du dein Praktikum gemacht?
Where did you do your work experience?

Ich habe (als)... gearbeitet.	I worked (as)...
in einem Geschäft	in a shop
in einem Büro	in an office
in einer Grundschule	in a primary school
in einer Praxis	in a surgery
in der Marketingabteilung	in the marketing department

Wie lange hast du da verbracht?
How long did you spend there?

Ich habe zwei Wochen da verbracht.
I spent two weeks there.

Was hast du gemacht?
What did you do?

Ich habe an der Kasse gearbeitet.
I worked on the till.

Ich habe das Telefon beantwortet.
I answered the telephone.

Ich habe kranken Leuten geholfen.
I helped ill people.

Ich habe mit Kindern / Tieren gearbeitet.
I worked with children / animals.

Wie fandest du das Praktikum?
How did you find the work experience?

Ich fand die Erfahrung...	I found the experience...
positiv ≠ negativ	positive ≠ negative
ganz toll	really great
eine Zeitverschwendung	a waste of time

Build Your Skills: Imperfect Modals

You can also use modal verbs to talk about the past:

Ich konnte die Tiere waschen.
I was able to wash the animals.

Du durftest mit den Kunden reden.
You were allowed to speak to the customers.

Er mochte gern die Verantwortung tragen.
He liked to bear the responsibility.

Wir mussten um sieben Uhr anfangen.
We had to start at seven o'clock.

Ihr solltet elegante Kleidung tragen.
You were supposed to wear smart clothes.

Sie wollten Erfahrungen sammeln.
They / You wanted to gain experience.

Jobs

Arzt / Ärztin	doctor
Bauer / Bäuerin	farmer
Bauarbeiter(in)	builder
Briefträger(in)	postman / postwoman
Elektriker(in)	electrician
Feuerwehrmann	firefighter
Friseur(in)	hairdresser
Fußballspieler(in)	football player
Informatiker(in)	IT specialist
Ingenieur(in)	engineer
Journalist(in)	journalist
Klempner(in)	plumber
Krankenpfleger / Krankenschwester	nurse (m. / f.)
Lehrer(in)	teacher
Mechaniker(in)	mechanic
Sänger(in)	singer
Schauspieler(in)	actor / actress
Sekretär(in)	secretary
Tierarzt / Tierärztin	vet (m. / f.)
Zahnarzt / Zahnärztin	dentist (m. / f.)

✓ Maximise Your Marks

In German you do not need to put an article before a job. You literally say 'I am babysitter', *not* 'I am *a* babysitter':
- **Ich bin Babysitterin.**

❓ Test Yourself

What do these mean in English?
1. **Ich habe mit Tieren gearbeitet.**
2. **Ich habe in einer Grundschule gearbeitet.**

How do you say these in German?
3. I worked as a vet in a surgery.
4. I spent three weeks there and I found the experience a waste of time.

⭐ Stretch Yourself

1. Say or write in English: '**Ich wollte in einer Schule arbeiten, aber ich durfte es nicht. Ich musste eine Woche in einem Büro verbringen.**'
2. Say or write in German: 'We spent two weeks in a shop and we had to speak to customers.'

Future Study and Career Plans

Future Career Plans

Was wirst du nach der Schule machen?
What will you do after school?

Ich will / werde / möchte...	I want / will / would like...
auf die Oberstufe gehen	to go into the sixth form
auf die Uni gehen	to go to university
eine Lehre machen	to do an apprenticeship
eine Arbeitsstelle finden	to find a good job
das Leben genießen	to enjoy life
meine Deutschkenntnisse verbessern	to improve my German language skills
in einem Team arbeiten	to work in a team
im Ausland arbeiten	to work abroad
(Lehrer) werden	to become a (teacher)

Modern Work Life

Man muss / kann / soll...	You have to / can / should...
sehr flexibel sein	be very flexible
einen Arbeitstisch teilen	share a desk
neue Aufgaben lernen	learn new tasks
durch E-Mails und Webinhalte kommunizieren	communicate via emails and web content
mit dem Chef / den Kollegen leicht in Kontakt bleiben	stay in easy contact with the boss / colleagues

Characteristics

Ein guter Zahnarzt ist immer / nie / oft / manchmal...	A good dentist is always / never / often / sometimes...
arrogant	arrogant
attraktiv	attractive
berühmt	famous
bescheiden	modest
ehrlich	honest
ernst	serious
fleißig	hard-working
geduldig	patient
gemein	mean
großartig	great
hilfsbereit	helpful
höflich	polite
humorlos	humourless
intelligent	intelligent
komisch	funny
locker	relaxed
ordentlich	organised
pünktlich	punctual
schüchtern	shy
selbstständig	independent
unfreundlich	unfriendly
unternehmungslustig	enterprising
zuverlässig	reliable
(immer) guter Laune	(always) in a good mood

✓ Maximise Your Marks

Use a range of adjectives in your written and spoken work. The examiner will be more impressed if you describe yourself as **unternehmungslustig** rather than **intelligent**.

Build Your Skills: Talking About the Future

Using a range of ways of expressing the future can greatly improve your speaking and writing marks. The infinitive (–en) is always at the end.

Ich werde mit sechzehn die Schule verlassen.
I will leave school at 16.

Ich möchte auf die Oberstufe gehen.
I would like to go into the sixth form.

Ich will einen Job finden.
I want to find a job.

Ich würde gern an der Uni studieren.
I would like to study at university.

Ich hoffe, viel Geld zu verdienen.
I hope to earn lots of money.

Applying for a Job

Before writing a letter of application in German, it is best to review all of the vocabulary and grammar in this topic and the personality traits from pages 14–15.

Here is an example of a typical job advertisement, letter of application and CV:

Sehr geehrte Damen und Herren,

ich möchte mich für den Ferienjob als Kellnerin in Ihrem Hotel bewerben. Ich habe die Anzeige in der ‚Tageszeitung' gelesen.

Ich besuche die Northolt-Gesamtschule in Südostengland und meine Lieblingsfächer sind Kunst und Fremdsprachen. Ich kann Deutsch, Pandschabi und ein bisschen Spanisch sprechen.

Ich habe bereits Erfahrungen als Kellnerin in einem Restaurant gesammelt und ich habe mein Praktikum in einem Supermarkt gemacht. Als Kellnerin musste ich immer freundlich und höflich sein und im Supermarkt war ich sehr hilfsbereit. Ich komme gut mit Kollegen und Kunden aus. Diese Eigenschaften finde ich sehr wichtig für eine Kellnerin in einem internationalen Hotel.

Bei Ihnen würde ich meine Berufserfahrungen erweitern und mein Deutsch verbessern.

Als Anlage schicke ich Ihnen meinen Lebenslauf und ich hoffe, bald von Ihnen zu hören.

Hochachtungsvoll

Daisy Patel

ANZEIGE

Wir brauchen Sie als Kellner(in) in unserem internationalen Hotel. Sie können Englisch in Wort und Schrift und haben noch andere Sprachkenntnisse. Restauranterfahrung erforderlich.

Schicken Sie uns Ihren Lebenslauf an: hr@hotel.de

Lebenslauf – Daisy Patel

Geburtsdatum: 16.09.1996

Geburtsort: Greenford, England

Schulabschlüsse: GCSE Englisch, Mathe, Naturwissenschaften, Deutsch, Kunst, Geschichte, Technologie, Religion

Berufserfahrung: Zwei Jahre als Kellnerin. Ich habe mein Praktikum in einem Supermarkt in London gemacht.

Eigenschaften: freundlich, hilfsbereit und sehr fleißig

Sonstiges: Ich bin sportlich und ich spiele in einer Schachmannschaft. Ich bin Klassensprecherin.

Build Your Skills: 'Um...Zu...' Constructions

The , **um...zu...** construction means 'in order to'. Whenever there is a phrase where you could say '(in order) to' in English, you *must* say it in German:

- I am going to university *to* study German.
  Ich gehe auf die Uni, um Deutsch zu studieren.

There is a comma before the **um** and there is an infinitive after the **zu** at the end of the sentence.

Another useful construction is , **ohne...zu...**, which means 'without doing something'. It follows the same rules as above.

- **Ich will viel Geld verdienen, ohne viel arbeiten zu müssen.**
  I want to earn lots of money *without* hav*ing to* work much.

? Test Yourself

Find the German for the following:

1. Dear Sir / Madam
2. I would like to apply for...
3. I have already gained experience as...
4. I find these characteristics very important for...
5. I am sending you my CV as an attachment.

★ Stretch Yourself

1. Say or write in English: '**Ich hoffe, eine Lehre zu machen, um eine gute Arbeitsstelle zu finden.**'
2. Say or write in German: 'I would like to go into the sixth form to study biology.'

Practice Questions

 Complete these exam-style questions to test your skills and understanding. Check your answers on pages 91–92. You may wish to answer these questions on a separate piece of paper.

Reading

1 Four students are writing about their school. Who do the statements below apply to? Hashem (H), Franz (F), Leevke (L) or Beate (B)? Write the correct letters in the boxes.

Ich liebe mein Gymnasium, weil es ganz neu ist. Die Lehrer sind auch total nett und helfen uns viel. Wir haben einen großen Computerraum, wo man auch Fremdsprachen online lernen kann. Mein Lieblingsfach ist Latein und in der Zukunft möchte ich im Ausland arbeiten. Letztes Jahr bin ich nach Spanien gefahren und es war unglaublich toll.

Leevke

Ich gehe nicht gern in meine Schule, weil die Lehrer keine Zeit für uns haben. Wir müssen fleißig arbeiten und Handys sind verboten. Unsere Schuluniform ist auch schrecklich. Wir dürfen keine Sportschuhe tragen.

Hashem

Mein Lieblingsfach ist Englisch und ich lese gern, aber unsere Bibliothek ist ziemlich alt und dreckig. Die Lehrer und Mitschüler sind manchmal hilfsbereit, aber ich hasse die Schule, weil ich sie zu stressig finde.

Beate

Meine Schule ist ziemlich erfolgreich, aber es gibt viele dumme Regeln. Wenn ich Schulleiter wäre, würde ich eine neue Schuluniform einführen, weil unsere Uniform furchtbar ist. Ich denke, dass man fleißig arbeiten muss, um eine gute Arbeitsstelle zu finden, aber es ist oft stressig in der Schule, weil die Lehrer sich nur für Prüfungen und gute Noten interessieren.

Franz

a) I have problems with the facilities at my school. ☐ (1)

b) At my school we can learn languages using the Internet. ☐ (1)

c) I would create a better school uniform for my school. ☐ (1)

d) My teachers are always too busy. ☐ (1)

e) I know what I want to do after leaving school. ☐ (1)

f) I find school stressful. ☐☐ (2)

g) I have problems with what we wear at school. ☐☐ (2)

Speaking

2 You have been asked to give a presentation about your working life. You will need to speak in German in full sentences, giving opinions and developing your answers where possible. Prepare your talk on the following points. When you are ready, record yourself on your phone.

   a) Describe your part-time job. Give five pieces of information.

   b) What will you do in the future after you have finished school? Why?

   c) What would you do if you were a millionaire? Why?

(10)

Writing

3 Your German friend on the social networking site 'Gesichtsbuch' wants to know about school life in your country. Write a short post about the following aspects. Give opinions too.

   * Give a description of your school, teachers and lessons.
   * Mention the school rules and your opinions of them.
   * Discuss the advantages and disadvantages of your school uniform. What would you wear in your dream school?

(15)

4 You have been asked to write an account about your work experience but it was *terrible*! Discuss this and the following work-related points and give opinions.

   * What did you do? How long did you spend there? How were your colleagues?
   * Describe your part-time job. How many hours do you work? How much do you get paid? Opinions?
   * Describe the job you would like to do in the future and why.

(15)

How well did you do?

| 0–12 | Try again | 13–24 | Getting there | 25–37 | Good work | 38–49 | Excellent! |

Music, Television, Film

Discussing Music

Was für Musik hörst du gern?
What kind of music do you like listening to?

Ich höre (nicht) gern...	I like (don't like) listening to...
(die) Heavymetal-Musik	heavy metal music
(die) klassische Musik	classical music
(die) Popmusik	pop music
(die) Rap-Musik	rap music

Warum hörst du Techno-Musik?
Why do you listen to techno music?

Sie ist...	It is...
rhythmisch	rhythmic
dynamisch	dynamic
lebhaft	lively
melodisch	melodic

Sie hat...	It has...
einen guten Beat	a good beat
einen Funkrhythmus	a funky rhythm

Wie kaufst du Musik?
How do you buy music?

Ich lade Musik aus dem Internet herunter.
I download music from the Internet.

Ich benutzte iTunes.	I use iTunes.
Ich kaufe CDs.	I buy CDs.

Ich tausche über Bluetooth Musik mit Freunden aus.
I share music with friends using Bluetooth.

MP3s sind billig.	MP3s are cheap.

Wann hörst du Musik?
When do you listen to music?

Ich höre morgens / abends Musik.
I listen to music in the mornings / in the evenings.

fast jeden Tag	almost every day
wenn ich unterwegs bin	when I'm on the move

Wo hörst du Musik?
Where do you listen to music?

Ich höre im Badezimmer Musik.
I listen to music in the bathroom.

im Schlafzimmer	in the bedroom
im Radio	on the radio
bei Freunden	at friends' houses
auf meinem Handy	on my mobile phone
auf einer Party	at a party

Asking Questions

Asking questions is easy in German. You simply swap the subject with the first verb of a sentence and add a question mark.

Er hört im Bad Musik.
He listens to music in the bath.

Hört er im Bad Musik?
Does he listen to music in the bath?

To ask more open questions, you add a question word to the beginning of the sentence:

Warum magst du DVDs?
Why do you like DVDs?

Wann hörst du Musik?
When do you listen to music?

Wie siehst du fern?
How do you watch television?

Wo siehst du dir Filme an?
Where do you watch films?

Was für Sendungen siehst du dir an?
What kind of programmes do you watch?

Discussing Television and Film

der Film	film
der Abenteuerfilm	adventure film
der Dokumentarfilm	documentary
der Fantasyfilm	fantasy film
der Horrorfilm	horror film
der Krimi	crime film
der Liebesfilm	love film
der Thriller	thriller
der Zeichentrickfilm	cartoon
die Sendung	programme
die Kindersendung	children's programme
die Musiksendung	music programme
die Quizsendung	quiz show
die Sportsendung	sports programme
die Tiersendung	animal programme
die Seifenoper	soap opera
die Komödie	comedy
die Nachrichten	news
das Drama	drama
Schauspieler(in)	actor / actress

Was ist deine Lieblingssendung?
What is your favourite programme?

Meine Lieblingssendung(en) ist / sind...
My favourite programme(s) is / are...

Mein(e) Lieblingsfilm(e) ist / sind...
My favourite film(s) is / are...

Seifenopern kann ich nicht leiden.
I can't stand soap operas.

Reviewing a Film

Ich habe gestern *Shrek* (im Kino) gesehen.
I watched *Shrek* (in the cinema) yesterday.

auf Blu-ray / DVD	on Blu-ray / DVD
im Fernsehen	on television

Das Hauptthema ist / war...	The main theme is / was...
(die) Liebe	love
(die) Gewalt	violence
(der) Mord	murder
(der) Tod	death
(die) Freiheit	freedom
Gut gegen Böse	good against evil

Die Spezialeffekte / Charaktere sind / waren...
The special effects / characters are / were...

Die Musik / Geschichte ist / war...	The music / story is / was...
eindrucksvoll	impressive
gewalttätig	violent
gruselig	creepy
kompliziert	complicated
romantisch	romantic
schrecklich	awful
spannend	exciting

Jack Black spielt die Rolle von...
Jack Black plays the role of...

Es geht um...   It is about...

Der Film findet in Mailand statt.
The film takes place in Milan.

✓ Maximise Your Marks

Understand the gist of tricky texts by first scanning for verbs, time and opinion words and vocabulary that you know and then put it into context.

? Test Yourself

What does this mean in English?
1. **Ich liebe Seifenopern, weil sie spannend und romantisch sind.**
2. **Die Geschichte war sehr kompliziert.**

How do you say these in German?
3. I like listening to classical music on the radio.
4. I can't stand documentaries.

★ Stretch Yourself

1. Say or write in English: '**Ich höre manchmal auf meinem Handy Rap-Musik und ich kaufe oft MP3s.**'
2. Say or write in German: 'Yesterday I watched *Jaws* on DVD. The story is quite complicated and it is about a big shark (**einen großen Hai**), who is called Jaws.'

New Media

Computer Language

der Bildschirm	screen
der Blog	blog
der Computer	computer
der Drucker	printer
der Punkt	dot
der Schrägstrich	forward slash
der Unterstrich	underscore
der Virus	virus
die E-Mail	email
die Maus	mouse
die Tastatur	keyboard
die Taste	key (of keyboard)
die Umfrage	survey / opinion poll
die Webseite	web page
die Verbindung	connection
das Internet	the Internet
das Kennwort	password
die Chatrooms	chat rooms
die Unterlagen	documents
online	online
Programmierer(in)	programmer
chatten	to chat
simsen	to text
*herunterladen	to download
*hochladen	to upload
im Internet surfen	to surf online
löschen	to delete
drucken	to print
speichern	to save

* separable verb

💡 Boost Your Memory

There are many words that are identical or similar in English and German (cognates). But beware! There are also some 'false friends'. These are words that look similar in the two languages but have different meanings. Make a list. For example:
- **Art** means 'kind' or 'type' in English.
- **bald** means 'soon'.
- **Beamer** means 'LCD projector'.
- **Brand** means 'fire'.
- **Chef** means 'boss'.

The Media in My Life

When describing your use of new media, you will probably want to use the present tense to describe actions that you do regularly. Review the present tense endings on page 18.

Was machst du am Computer?
What do you do on the computer?

Ich schreibe mein Online-Profil.
I write my online profile.

Du spielst am Computer. You play on the computer.

Er lädt Fotos hoch. He uploads photos.

Sie tauscht Videos aus. She shares videos.

Wir schreiben und lesen E-Mails.
We write and read emails.

Ihr benutzt MySpace. You use MySpace.

Sie surfen im Internet. They surf online.

Sie können mit dem Handy fotografieren.
You can take photos with your mobile phone.

Build Your Skills: Structuring Arguments

A well-structured and balanced response is crucial for obtaining the highest marks in written work. Your responses should follow a logical order. Here is one way to structure your ideas:

1. State some advantages of a topic first:
   Die neuen Medien haben viele Vorteile.
   There are a lot of advantages of new media.
2. Then state some disadvantages:
   Die Nachteile sind deutlich zu sehen.
   The disadvantages are clear to see.
3. Use sequencers to introduce each point:
   erstens (firstly), **zweitens** (secondly), **dann** (then), **danach** (after that), **zum Schluss** (finally), **einerseits** (on the one hand), **andererseits** (on the other hand)
   Remember to keep the verb in second place.
4. Finish with your own opinion and justify it using **weil** or **denn**:
   Zum Schluss denke ich, dass... (verb).
   Finally, I think that...

Pros and Cons of New Media

Extending your responses to include different views or opinions will get you higher marks in speaking and writing. You will also need to recognise views and opinions in reading and listening tasks. Here are some viewpoints about new media:

Vorteile (Advantages) ✓

Man kann...	You can...
online fernsehen	watch television online
mit Freunden aus aller Welt in Kontakt bleiben	remain in contact with friends from around the world
mit dem Computer Zeit sparen	save time with a computer
Informationen schnell finden	find information quickly
auf dem Handy Zeitungen lesen	read newspapers on your mobile

Das Internet hilft beim Studium.
The Internet helps your studies.

E-Mails zu schicken ist einfach und billig.
Sending emails is easy and cheap.

Nachteile (Disadvantages) ✗

Man verbringt weniger Zeit mit Freunden.
You spend less time with friends.

Das Internet ist gefährlich.
The Internet is dangerous.

Junge Leute sind in Chatrooms nicht immer sicher.
Young people are not always safe in chat rooms.

Es gibt zu viele unkontrollierte Sex-Webseiten.
There are too many uncontrolled sex websites.

Neue Technologien sind teuer und nicht immer zuverlässig.
New technologies are expensive and not always reliable.

Viele junge Leute sind <u>wegen</u> Videospielen faul geworden.
Many young people have become lazy <u>because</u> of video games.

Sie sind vom Handy / von der Konsole abhängig.
They are addicted to their mobile phone / console.

Expressing Your Opinions

Get your opinions across in a variety of ways:

- Use these expressions:

Ich denke, dass... (verb).	I think that...
Ich glaube, dass... (verb).	I believe that...
Meiner Meinung nach...	In my opinion...
Ich finde...	I find...
Ich stimme (+ dative)**...zu**	I agree with...
Ich bin (nicht) damit einverstanden.	I (don't) agree with that.
Es kommt darauf an.	It depends.

- Use more complex opinion words in your work:
  unmöglich (impossible), **unsicher** (uncertain), **entsetzlich** (appalling), **bestimmt** (definite), **typisch** (typical)

- Add extra emotion in your sentences by using intensifiers. The verb must come second if you start with these:
  wirklich (really), **wahrscheinlich** (probably), **vielleicht** (maybe), **völlig** (completely), **total** (totally), **eigentlich** (actually)

? Test Yourself

What does this mean in English?
1. **Meiner Meinung nach ist das Internet total gefährlich.**
2. **Ich tausche Fotos und Musik aus.**

How do you say these in German?
3. You can find information quickly. (**Man**)
4. You can text with your mobile phone. (**Sie**)

★ Stretch Yourself

1. Say or write in English: '**Ich glaube, dass die neuen Medien viele Vorteile haben. Erstens kann man Unterlagen online speichern. Zweitens kann man Zeit mit dem Internet sparen.**'

2. Say or write in German: 'On the other hand, the disadvantages are clear to see: young people have become addicted to uncontrolled chat rooms. In my opinion the Internet is probably dangerous, but I surf online every day.'

Clothes and Fashion

Clothes and Accessories

Clothing words are useful when describing people. Review the items of clothing on page 28 first. Here is some more vocabulary.

Was trägst du gern?   What do you like wearing?

Ich trage (nicht) gern...	I (don't) like wearing / carrying...
einen Anzug	a suit
einen Bademantel	a bathrobe
einen BH (Büstenhalter)	a bra
einen Gürtel	a belt
einen Hut	a hat
einen (Regen)Mantel	a (rain)coat
einen Rucksack	a rucksack
einen Schal	a scarf
einen Schlafanzug	pyjamas
einen Slip	knickers
einen Sportanzug	a tracksuit
eine Armbanduhr	a watch
eine Badehose	trunks
eine Halskette	a necklace
eine Handtasche	a handbag
eine Mütze	a cap
eine Sonnenbrille	(a pair of) sunglasses
eine Strickjacke	a cardigan
eine Strumpfhose	tights
eine Tätowierung	a tattoo
eine Unterhose	a pair of underpants
ein Nachthemd	a nightie
ein Portemonnaie	a purse
Handschuhe	gloves
Hausschuhe / Pantoffeln	slippers
Sandalen	sandals

✓ Maximise Your Marks

For the highest accuracy and range of language marks you need to include a variety of adjectives in your work and ensure that the endings on your articles and adjectives are correct and correspond to the gender, case and preposition. Review adjective endings on page 28. For example:

- **Am Wochenende trage ich ein kurzes, bequemes Top mit einer kleinen, schwarzen Handtasche.**
  At the weekend I wear a short, comfortable top with a small, black handbag.

Talking About Clothes

(aus) Wolle	(made of) wool
(aus) Baumwolle	(made of) cotton
(aus) Leder	(made of) leather
(aus) Seide	(made of) silk
(aus) Kunststoff	(made of) plastic

bequem	comfortable
ethisch	ethical
lässig	casual
schick	trendy
günstig	reasonable / cheap
preiswert	good value
modisch	fashionable
gestreift	striped
kariert	checked

Es steht dir gut.	It suits you.

Your Look

Gehörst du zu einer Gruppe?
Do you belong to a group?

Ich bin ein Emo / Grufti / Punk / Skater / Individualist.
I am an emo / goth / punk / skater / individual.

Ich bin weder Punk noch Grufti.
I am neither a punk nor a goth.

Das Leben als Emo ist ein gutes Leben und ich gehöre dazu.
The emo life is a good life and I belong to it.

Wie siehst du aus?
How do you look?

Wir tragen Schwarz.
We dress in black.

Wir haben eine Frisur mit langem Pony im Gesicht.
We have a hairstyle with a long fringe in our face.

Ich habe eine Tätowierung und viele Piercings.
I have a tattoo and lots of piercings.

Fashion Opinions

Was hältst du von Gruftis?
What do you think about goths?

Sie sehen alle gleich aus.
They all look the same.

Ich sehe lieber anders aus.
I prefer to look different.

Diese Gruppen finde ich blöd, weil…
I find these groups stupid, because…

Ich habe (keine) Lust, zu einer Gruppe zu gehören.
I (don't) feel like belonging to a group.

Zu einer Gruppe zu gehören macht viel Spaß, weil…
Belonging to a group is a lot of fun, because…

Meiner Meinung nach ist das langweilig, weil…
In my opinion that is boring, because…

Ich interessiere mich (nicht) für…	I'm (not) interested in…
die neuesten Trends	the latest trends
die teuersten Marken	the most expensive brands
die passenden Accessoires	matching accessories

Build Your Skills: More 'Kicking Words'

Justify and contrast your opinions as often as possible. Use **weil** (because) and other subordinating conjunctions (see page 27) to do this. Remember, the first verb is kicked to the end of the sentence. Here are some more 'kicking words':

was (what), **wie** (how), **ob** (whether), **bis** (until), **damit** (so that), **nachdem** (after), **da** (as / since).

- **Ich trage genau das**, was **ich tragen** will.
  I wear exactly what I want to wear.
- **Meine Haare sind nicht mehr schwarz**, nachdem **ich ein Foto von mir gesehen** habe.
  My hair is no longer black, after I saw a photo of myself.
- **Wir kommen oft zum Skatepark**, damit **wir einander neue Tricks beibringen** können.
  We often come to the skate park, so that we can teach each other new tricks.

Past and Future Fashion

You can use a range of tenses in your work when talking about fashion. This gives your writing and speaking more depth.

Past

Früher habe ich nur Sportanzüge getragen. Ich habe sehr sportlich ausgesehen.
In the past I wore only tracksuits. I looked very sporty.

Present

Heutzutage trage ich T-Shirts mit Logos, coole Mützen und einen Kopfhörer.
Nowadays I wear T-shirts with logos, cool caps and headphones.

Future

Ich weiß nicht, wie ich in fünf Jahren aussehen werde. Vielleicht werde ich Anzüge tragen.
I don't know how I will look in five years. Perhaps I will wear suits.

? Test Yourself

What do these mean in English?
1. Emokinder sehen alle gleich aus.
2. Ich interessiere mich nicht für passende Accessoires.

How do you say these in German?
3. I like wearing sunglasses and a hat.
4. I am a goth and we dress in black.

★ Stretch Yourself

1. Say or write in English: '**Damit ich immer anders aussehe, werde ich morgen einen teuren Schal aus Wolle kaufen. Früher habe ich mich für die neuesten Trends und Marken nicht interessiert.**'

2. Say or write in German: 'The goth life is good and I belong to it. We wear black jeans and long, black coats. I have many piercings and a tattoo, since they are really cool.'

Shopping

Shops

der Laden	shop	die Buchhandlung	book shop
der Blumenladen	florist's	die Drogerie	(non-dispensing) chemist
der Fischhändler	fishmonger's		
der Markt	market	die Fleischerei / der Fleischer	butcher's
der Obst- und Gemüsehändler	greengrocer's	die Metzgerei / der Metzger	butcher's
der Supermarkt	supermarket	die Konditorei	cake shop
der Tante-Emma-Laden	corner shop	das Einkaufszentrum	shopping centre
der (Zeitungs)kiosk	(newspaper) kiosk	das Elektrogeschäft	electrical shop
die Apotheke	chemist's	das Juweliergeschäft	jeweller's
die Bäckerei / der Bäcker	baker's	das Kaufhaus / Warenhaus	department store

Leisure and Lifestyle

Shopping Preferences

Wo gehst du *einkaufen?
Where do you go shopping'?

Ich kaufe oft auf dem Flohmarkt ein.
I often shop at flea markets.

Er kauft meistens im Internet ein.
He shops mostly on the Internet.

Früher habe ich in der Bäckerei eingekauft.
In the past I shopped at the baker's.

Bald werde ich im Bioladen einkaufen.
Soon I will shop at the organic food shop.

Was kauft man dort?
What do you buy there?

Wir kaufen Badeanzüge im Modeladen.
We buy bathing costumes in the fashion store.

Ich kaufe Socken in der Kinderabteilung.
I buy socks in the children's department.

* separable verb

Man kann alles im Einkaufszentrum kaufen.
You can buy everything in the shopping centre.

Ich gehe (nicht so) gern einkaufen.
I (don't much) like going shopping.

nur selten / so oft wie möglich / zweimal pro Jahr
very rarely / as often as possible / twice a year

✓ Maximise Your Marks

Remember, when using the prepositions **in** (in) and **bei** (at), you need to use the dative case if there is no movement involved. (Look back at prepositions and the dative on page 30.)

Masculine: **der Bäcker** ➡ **beim Bäcker**
Feminine: **die Metzgerei** ➡ **in der Metzgerei**
Neuter: **das Kaufhaus** ➡ **im Kaufhaus**

im is short for **in dem**
beim is short for **bei dem**

Demonstrative Adjectives

Demonstrative adjectives say if something is near to or far from the speaker. They take the same endings as the definite article (see page 30).

dieser Laden / **diese** Läden   this shop / these shops
jener   that / those
welcher?   which? / what?

Adjectives that follow the same ending pattern are: **jeder** (every), **jeglicher** (any), **mancher** (some), **solcher** (such)

- **Dieser Laden ist teuer.**
  This shop is expensive.
- **Welches Geschäft ist billig?**
  Which shop is cheap?
- **Manche Kaufhäuser sind zu groß.**
  Some department stores are too big.

Build Your Skills: Opinions About Shopping

For higher grades you need to give points of view and justify your answers. Here are some useful opinion words and phrases for shopping:

Einkaufen ist mein Leben / größtes Hobby.
Shopping is my life / biggest hobby.

Mir ist der Preis besonders wichtig.
The price is really important to me.

Mir ist das Label gar nicht wichtig.
The label is not at all important to me.

In der Konditorei gibt es immer Qualität zu niedrigen Preisen.
At the cake shop there is always quality at low prices.

Das Modegeschäft verkauft stark reduzierte Kleidung direkt aus der Fabrik.
The fashion store sells greatly reduced clothes straight from the factory.

Vor drei Jahren war ich einkaufssüchtig und ich musste die neuesten Modetrends kaufen.
Three years ago I was addicted to shopping and I had to buy the latest fashion trends.

Einige Leute sind verrückt nach Einkaufen, aber ich verstehe das einfach nicht.
Some people are crazy about shopping, but I just don't understand that.

Einkaufen ist eine Zeitverschwendung und ist irrsinnig langweilig.
Shopping is a waste of time and is mind-bogglingly boring.

Ich kaufe immer im Internet ein, weil ich mir nur billige Produkte leisten kann.
I always shop online, because I can only afford cheap products.

Shopping Vocabulary

das Sonderangebot	special offer
der Rabatt	discount
die Ermäßigung	reduction
der Schlussverkauf	sale
das Pfand	deposit
die Münze	coin
das Kleingeld	change
der Geldschein	note
der Euro	euro
der Cent	cent
das Pfund	pound sterling
geschlossen	shut
geöffnet	open
der Ruhetag	closing day
ausverkauft	sold out
die Kasse	cash till / checkout
niedrig ≠ hoch	low ≠ high
billig ≠ teuer	cheap ≠ expensive

More Question Words

Here are some more question words related to shopping. See also page 40.

Wie viel?	How much? / How many?
Wie?	How?
Wer?	Who?
Wie oft?	How often?

Take care not to confuse **wer** (who) with **wo** (where).

Wie viel kostet es?
How much does it cost?

Wie groß ist der Markt?
How big is the market?

Wer verkauft Rhabarbermarmelade?
Who sells rhubarb jam?

Wie oft gehst du einkaufen?
How often do you go shopping?

? Test Yourself

What do these mean in English?
1. Ich gehe nicht gern einkaufen.
2. Dieser Laden ist billig.

How do you say these in German?
3. florist's, sale, organic food shop
4. Which book shop? That book shop!

★ Stretch Yourself

1. Say or write in English: 'Einige Leute sind verrückt nach Schlussverkäufen, aber Einkaufen ist nicht mein größtes Hobby.'
2. Say or write in German: 'I often shop at the organic food shop, because price is not important to me.'

Events and Celebrations

Celebrations, Events and Holidays

der Event	event
der Geburtstag	birthday
der Feiertag	public holiday
der Heiligabend	Christmas Eve
die Feier	celebration
die Hochzeit	wedding
die Party	party
die Überraschungsparty	surprise party
die Weihnachtsfeier	Christmas party
die Taufe	baptism
die Geburt	birth
die Beerdigung	funeral
die Ferien	the holidays
die Verlobung	engagement
die Faschingsfete	Fasching party
Fasching / Karneval	carnival (February)
Silvester	New Year's Eve
Pfingsten	Whitsun
Weihnachten	Christmas
Ostern	Easter
das Jubiläum	anniversary
das Oktoberfest	Oktoberfest festival
das Volksfest	folk festival
das Konzert	concert
das Grillfest	barbeque party
das Picknick	picnic
das (Pokal)Endspiel	(cup) final (sports event)

Past Participles

A past participle is used in the perfect tense (see page 34) and the pluperfect tense, which both describe events that have finished in the past. German past participles need to be learned with their infinitive, as many are irregular.

Past participles cannot be used alone. They need an auxiliary verb before them. This is usually a form of **haben**, but is sometimes **sein**. See below for some examples:

feiern	to celebrate	➡	gefeiert
*einladen	to invite	➡	eingeladen
*vorbereiten	to prepare	➡	vorbereitet
essen	to eat	➡	gegessen
trinken	to drink	➡	getrunken
tanzen	to dance	➡	getanzt
singen	to sing	➡	gesungen
plaudern	to chat	➡	geplaudert
organisieren	to organise	➡	organisiert
*kennenlernen	to get to know	➡	kennengelernt
**gehen	to go	➡	gegangen
**fahren	to travel	➡	gefahren

* separable verbs ** verbs that take **sein**

💡 Boost Your Memory

When learning a new verb, always write down its past participle too and whether it takes **haben** or **sein**. This will save you time in the future and means that you will be able to put that verb in any perfect tense.

Build Your Skills: The Pluperfect Tense

The pluperfect tense is used to describe events that *had* happened before another event happened. It is made up of two parts:

> the imperfect (simple past) tense of **haben** or **sein** (see page 64) + a past participle

The events below had all happened before...
Meine Mutti ist ins Bett gegangen.
My mum went to bed.

Mein Vater hatte eine Überraschungsparty für Mutti organisiert.
My dad had organised a surprise party for my mother.

Meine Tante hatte viele Gäste eingeladen.
My aunt had invited lots of guests.

Wir waren **in den Supermarkt** gegangen **und** hatten **einen Kuchen** gekauft.
We had gone to the supermarket and had bought a cake.

Wir hatten **laut** gesungen **und** hatten **wie Idioten** getanzt.
We had sung loudly and had danced like idiots.

💡 Boost Your Memory

Think of the pluperfect tense as the past of the past. It talks about actions further back in time than another action in the past. Remember that verbs which take **sein** need to take an imperfect form of **sein**. 'I had gone' in German is like saying 'I was gone' ➡ **Ich war gegangen.**

Using a Range of Tenses

Using a range of tenses in your written and spoken work and recognising them in reading and listening activities is crucial. The more tenses you learn and can use, the higher your grade should be. If you can use up to three tenses well, then you could get a Grade C or above.

Present Tense
- **Das Oktoberfest** findet **jedes Jahr in München** statt.
  The Oktoberfest festival takes place every year in Munich.
- **Es** gibt **Bierzelte, Imbissstuben, Musik und einen Festzug.**
  There are beer tents, snack bars, music and a procession.

Perfect Tense
- **Ich** bin **zum ersten Mal letzten Herbst** <u>dorthin</u> gefahren.
  I went <u>there</u> last autumn for the first time.
- **Wir** haben **Bratwurst** gegessen **und es** hat **jede Menge Spaß** gemacht.
  We ate fried sausage and had loads of fun.

Future Tense
- **Nächstes Jahr** werde ich **die Volksmusik** aufnehmen.
  Next year I will record the German folk music.

Modal Verbs
- **Man** kann **Bier** trinken **und heimische Spezialitäten** probieren.
  You can drink beer and try local specialities.

Imperfect Tense (Simple Past)
- **Es** gab **ein großes Feuerwerk und es** war **sehr laut.**
  There was a large firework display and it was very loud.
- **Die Band** spielte **Musik und ich** fand **das einmalig.**
  The band was playing music and I found it unique.

Pluperfect Tense
- **Mein Vater** war **1970** <u>da</u> gewesen **und er** hatte **mir ein Foto** <u>davon</u> gezeigt.
  My father had been <u>there</u> in 1970 and he had shown me a photo <u>of it</u>.

Subjunctive and Conditional Mood
- **Wenn ich 18 Jahre alt** wäre, würde ich **zwei Maß Bier** trinken.
  If I were 18 years old, I would drink two litres of beer.
- **Ich** möchte **unbedingt wieder dahin** fahren. **Ich** würde **eine ganze Gans** essen.
  I would definitely like to go back there. I would eat a whole goose.

❓ Test Yourself

Change **feiern** and **tanzen** into the **ich** form of these tenses:
1 Present tense
2 Perfect tense
3 Future tense

⭐ Stretch Yourself

Change **organisieren** and **fahren** into the **ich** form of these tenses:
1 Perfect tense
2 Pluperfect tense

Sports and Pastimes

Sports

Was ist deine Lieblingssportart?
What is your favourite type of sport?

Meine Lieblingssportart ist...	My favourite type of sport is...
Badminton / Federball	badminton
Fußball	football
Golf	golf
Gymnastik	gymnastics
Handball	handball
Leichtathletik	athletics
Tennis	tennis
Tischtennis	table tennis

Ich treibe keinen Sport.
I don't do any sport.

Sport ist Mord!
Sport is a killer!

You can take the infinitive of the sport verb, e.g. **laufen** (to run), and use it as a noun by giving it a capital letter: **Laufen** (running).

Angeln	fishing
Boxen	boxing
Fallschirmspringen	parachuting
Joggen	jogging
Kegeln	bowling
Klettern	climbing
Radfahren	cycling
Reiten	riding
Rollschuhlaufen	roller-skating
Schwimmen	swimming
Segeln	sailing
Skilaufen	skiing
Snowboarden	snowboarding
Tanzen	dancing
Trainieren	training
Wandern	hiking
Windsurfen	windsurfing

Pastimes

Time and frequency words are very important in listening and reading activities, as they are often key to your understanding. Including time and frequency words in your sentences also adds interest to your work. The German time and frequency words below are underlined.

Was machst du gern in deiner Freizeit?
What do you like doing in your free time?

Ich chatte gern mit Freunden online.
I like chatting with friends online.

Ich lese im Bus Romane. I read novels on the bus.
Ich chille mit Freunden. I chill with friends.

Wie oft machst du das? How often do you do that?

Ich faulenze ab und zu. I laze around now and then.
Ich ruhe mich selten aus. I rarely relax.
Ich gehe oft auf Partys. I often go to parties.

Ich gehe nie mit Freunden aus.
I never go out with friends.

Ich höre immer Musik.
I always listen to music.

Ich sehe abends fern.
I watch TV in the evenings.

Ich übe häufig ein Instrument.
I often practise an instrument.

Ich treibe regelmäßig Sport.
I do sport regularly.

Ich spiele täglich Computerspiele.
I play computer games daily.

Ich spiele morgens mit der Band.
I play with the band in the mornings.

Ich sammle Briefmarken.
I collect stamps.

Ich telefoniere jedes Wochenende.
I phone every weekend.

✓ Maximise Your Marks

When time or frequency words are in the middle of a sentence they always come directly after the first verb or after the subject if the first verb has been kicked to the end of the sentence.

Build Your Skills: Past and Future Interests

Contrasting things you have done with things you will or would like to do is a great way to develop a response. Remember to give opinions too.

Letztes Jahr habe ich Angeln probiert, aber es war langweilig.
Last year I tried fishing, but it was boring.

Ich würde gern Bogenschießen probieren, weil das cool aussieht.
I would like to try archery, because it looks cool.

In der Grundschule habe ich täglich Blockflöte gespielt.
At primary school I played the recorder daily.

Wenn ich älter bin, werde ich sicher mal Dudelsack probieren.
When I am older I will definitely try the bagpipes.

Vorgestern sind wir durch den Wald gelaufen.
The day before yesterday we ran through the woods.

Ich fand das total anstrengend, da wir schnell gelaufen sind.
I found it totally exhausting, as we ran quickly.

Übermorgen würde ich gern einen Berg besteigen.
The day after tomorrow I would like to climb a mountain.

Musical Instruments

To say what instrument you play, omit the 'the' and just say the instrument.

> **Spielst du ein Instrument?**
> Do you play an instrument?

Ich spiele kein Instrument.
I don't play any instrument.

Ich spiele (mittwochs) Schlagzeug.
I play drums (on Wednesdays).

(die) Blockflöte	recorder
(die) Geige	violin
(die) (E-)Gitarre	(electric) guitar
(die) Flöte	flute
(die) Klarinette	clarinette
(die) Trompete	trumpet
(das) Cello	cello
(das) Klavier	piano

Build Your Skills: 'Als' or 'Wenn'?

Als and **wenn** both mean 'when' in English and both kick the first verb to the end of the clause.

Als is used when you are talking about an action in the past:
- Als **ich im Zug** war, habe **ich mein Buch** gelesen.
  When I was on the train, I read my book.

Wenn is used for present tense actions:
- Wenn **ich das Geld** habe, gehe **ich in Northolt schwimmen.**
  When I have the money, I go swimming in Northolt.

Remember the subordinate clause rule on page 31.

❓ Test Yourself

What do these mean in English?
1. **Ich tanze jedes Wochenende.**
2. **Ich übe häufig Geige.**

How do you say these in German?
3. I play the trumpet daily.
4. My favourite type of sport is cycling.

⭐ Stretch Yourself

1. Say or write in English: **'Als ich in der Grundschule war, bin ich oft auf Partys gegangen.'**
2. Say or write in German: 'I have been practising the piano for two years, but I would like to try the bagpipes.'

Build Your Skills: Using 'Seit'

To say how long you *have been doing* something you need to use the word **seit** (since / for) with the present tense. It requires the dative case after it:

Seit wann spielst **du Golf?**
How long have you been playing golf?

Ich spiele seit **den Ferien Golf.**
I have been playing golf since the holidays.

Wir chatten seit **einer Stunde online.**
We have been chatting online for an hour.

Food and Drink

Food

Was isst du (nicht) gern?
What do you (not) like eating?

Ich esse (nicht) gern...	I (don't) like eating...
das Gemüse	vegetables
der Blumenkohl	cauliflower
der Kohl	cabbage
der Knoblauch	garlic
der Rosenkohl	Brussel sprouts
der Salat	salad / lettuce
der Spinat	spinach
die Erbsen	peas
die grünen Bohnen	green beans
die Gurke	cucumber
die Karotte	carrot
die Kartoffeln	potatoes
die Pilze / Champignons	mushrooms
die Zwiebel	onion
das Sauerkraut	pickled cabbage
das Obst	fruit
der Apfel	apple
der Pfirsich	peach
die Ananas	pineapple
die Aprikose	apricot
die Banane	banana
die Birne	pear
die Erdbeere	strawberry
die Himbeere	raspberry
die Kirsche	cherry
die Orange	orange
die Pampelmuse	grapefruit
die Pflaume	plum
die Tomate	tomato
die Weintraube	grape
die Zitrone	lemon
das Fleisch	meat
der Aufschnitt	assorted cold meats
der Braten	roast
der Hamburger	hamburger
der Schinken	ham
der Truthahn	turkey
die Bratwurst	fried sausage
die Currywurst	curry sausage
die Ente	duck
die Frikadelle	meatball / burger
die Leberwurst	liver sausage

die Wurst	sausage
das Hähnchen	chicken
das Kalbfleisch	veal
das Rindfleisch	beef
das Schaschlik	kebab
das Schnitzel	Schnitzel
das Schweinefleisch	pork
das Steak	steak
der Fisch	fish
die Forelle	trout
der Thunfisch	tuna
der Lachs	salmon
die Meeresfrüchte	seafood
die Eier	eggs
das gekochte Ei	boiled egg
das Rührei	scrambled egg
das Spiegelei	fried egg
der Reis	rice
die Chips	crisps
die Haferflocken	porridge
die Suppe	soup
das Brot	bread
das Brötchen	roll
das Butterbrot	sandwich
die Nudeln	noodles
die Pommes (frites)	chips
das Bonbon	boiled sweet
der Kuchen	cake
der Käse	cheese
die Kekse	biscuits
die Schokolade	chocolate
die (Schlag)Sahne	(whipped) cream
die Torte	tart / flan
das Eis	ice-cream
die Süßigkeiten	sweets

💡 Boost Your Memory

Learn vocabulary together with bright and colourful images as this strengthens your memory. For example, why not write the word **Erbsen** (peas) within six bright green peas and the word **Kohl** (cabbage) within a big plate of cabbage.

Leisure and Lifestyle

Drink

Was trinkst du (nicht) gern?
What do you (not) like drinking?

Ich trinke (nicht) gern...	I (don't) like drinking...
der Fruchtsaft ⬇	fruit juice
der Kaffee	coffee
der Kakao	cocoa
der (Kräuter)Tee	(herbal) tea
der (Orangen)Saft	(orange) juice
der Wein	wine
die Cola	cola
die Limonade	lemonade
die (Voll)Milch	(full fat / whole) milk
das Bier	beer
das Pils	lager
das Wasser	water

Build Your Skills: Quantities

Extend your answers by adding extra details. You do not need a word for 'of' in German when discussing quantities.
For example: **eine Flasche Cola** (a bottle of cola).

eine Dose	a tin / can
ein paar	a few
eine Flasche	a bottle
ein Glas	a glass
ein Kännchen	a pot
ein Liter	a litre
eine Packung	a pack
eine Portion	a portion
eine Schachtel	a box
eine Scheibe	a slice
ein Stück(chen)	a (little) piece
eine Tasse	a cup
eine Tüte	a bag
eine Menge	loads of

✔ Maximise Your Marks

You can also extend your answers by adding time and frequency words, quantities, extra details about food such as **mit...** (with...) or **ohne...** (without...), different tenses, opinions and reasons.

Eating and Drinking Habits

Try to extend your answers to every question. Repeat some of the question in your answer to make it longer:
- **Was isst du zu Mittag?**
  What do you eat for lunch?
- **Zu Mittag esse ich Pasteten.**
  For lunch I eat pies.

zum Frühstück	for breakfast
zum Mittagessen	for lunch
zum Abendessen	for dinner
in der Pause	at break
zwischendurch	(in)between meals
an einem typischen Tag	on a typical day
als Vorspeise	as a starter
als Hauptgericht	as a main course
als Nachspeise / Nachtisch	as pudding / dessert

Das finde ich (zu)...	I find that (too)...		
salzig	salty	süß	sweet
scharf	spicy	roh	raw
hart	hard	köstlich	delicious
lecker	tasty	fettig	fatty / greasy
frisch	fresh	ekelhaft	disgusting

❓ Test Yourself

What do these mean in English?
1. Als Vorspeise möchte ich die Forelle.
2. Ich trinke nicht gern Apfelsaft. Er ist zu süß.
How do you say these in German?
3. I like eating curry sausage with chips.
4. For breakfast I eat porridge with milk.

⭐ Stretch Yourself

1. Say or write in English: '**Als Hauptgericht habe ich grüne Bohnen und eine Scheibe Schinken gegessen.**'
2. Say or write in German: 'Between meals I like eating a piece of cake with cream. I find that very tasty.'

Health and Fitness

Impersonal Verbs

An impersonal verb represents an action where there is no subject. These verbs start with the impersonal pronoun **es** (it) and are commonly used to talk about the weather: **Es regnet.** (It's raining.)

Include some impersonal verbs in your work for added complexity.

Es tut mir weh. It hurts.
Es geht mir schlecht. I feel ill.
Was ist geschehen? What happened?

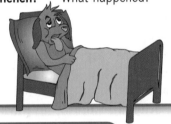

Pains and Aches

Was tut weh? What hurts?
Der Bauch tut mir weh. My belly hurts.

der Arm	arm	die Schulter	shoulder
der Finger	finger	die Nase	nose
der Fuß	foot	das Bein	leg
der Hals	neck	das Gehirn	brain
der Kopf	head	das Handgelenk	wrist
der Körper	body	das Herz	heart
der Magen	stomach	das Kinn	chin
der Mund	mouth	das Knie	knee
der Rücken	back	das Ohr	ear
der Zahn	tooth	die Augen	eyes
die Hand	hand		

Ich bin krank.	I am ill.
Ich habe...	I have...
Bauchschmerzen	belly ache
Rückenschmerzen	backache
Kopfschmerzen	a headache
Ohrenschmerzen	earache
Halsschmerzen	a sore throat
Zahnschmerzen	toothache
Durchfall	diarrhoea
Fieber	a temperature
Schnupfen	a cold
Husten	a cough
die Grippe	flu

Build Your Skills: More Adjective Endings

Using a variety of adjectives in your work gains you higher marks. When an adjective comes before a noun, it must agree with the number, gender and case of the noun. This is done by changing the ending of the adjective.

The table shows the adjective endings to use after the definite article **der** (the) and after **dieser** (this), **jener** (that), **jeder** (every), **mancher** (some), **solcher** (such) and **welcher** (which).

	Masc.	Fem.	Neuter	Plural
Nom.	der linke Arm	die linke Hand	das linke Bein	die weißen Zähne
Accu.	den linken Arm	die linke Hand	das linke Bein	die weißen Zähne
Dat.	dem linken Arm	der linken Hand	dem linken Bein	den weißen Zähnen

See page 28 for adjective endings used after **ein**, **kein**, **mein**, etc.

Ich habe mir letztes Jahr das rechte Handgelenk gebrochen.
I broke my right wrist last year.

Ich habe mir mit dem großen Messer in die linke Hand geschnitten.
I cut my left hand with the big knife.

Ich habe mir gestern den rechten Fuß verstaucht / verletzt.
I sprained / injured my right foot yesterday.

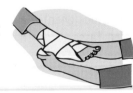

💡 Boost Your Memory

One way of remembering the adjective endings is to think of a butcher's knife resting on a chopping board (see the shaded area in the table above). The endings around the knife are all the same: **–en**, and the endings within the knife have been chopped off, leaving just **–e**.

Healthy and Unhealthy Lifestyles

Bist du sportlich / gesund / ungesund?
Are you sporty / healthy / unhealthy?

Ich bin (un)fit / aktiv / übergewichtig / sportscheu.
I am (un)fit / active / overweight / unsporty.

Ich gehe dreimal in der Woche zum Training.
I go to training three times a week.

Sport fällt mir schwer, weil ich unfit bin.
I find sport difficult, because I am unfit.

Ich mache Aerobic und trainiere jeden Tag.
I do aerobics and train every day.

Ernährst du dich gesund / ungesund?
Do you eat healthily / unhealthily?

Ich bin eine Naschkatze.
I have a sweet tooth.

Ich bin ein Stubenhocker.
I am a couch potato.

Ich bin Vegetarier(in).
I am a vegetarian.

Um stark und gesund zu sein, (verb)...
In order to be strong and healthy,...

Um in Form zu bleiben, (verb)...
In order to keep in shape,...

eine ausgewogene Ernährung
a balanced diet

Ein gutes Frühstück ist äußerst wichtig.
A good breakfast is crucial.

Süße Getränke trinke ich nie.
I never drink sweet drinks.

Ich esse gern Obst und Gemüse.
I like eating fruit and vegetables.

Wie kommst du zur Schule?
How do you get to school?

Ich fahre mit dem Auto, weil das so schnell ist.
I travel by car, because it is so quick.

Ich fahre mit dem Rad, weil das entspannend ist.
I cycle, because it is relaxing.

Build Your Skills: Giving Advice Using Modal Verbs

As well as developing your answers and giving opinions to gain higher marks, there is a good opportunity within the topic of health and fitness to give advice on a situation. To say what people could or should do to stay fit, use the imperfect subjunctive mood of **können** (to be able to) and **sollen** (to be supposed to). You need the imperfect tense endings for this:

Ich sollte **weniger Fastfood essen.**
I should eat less fast food.

Du könntest **mit dem Rad fahren.**
You could cycle.

Man sollte **keinen Alkohol trinken.**
You should not drink any alcohol.

Wir könnten **mehr Gemüse kochen.**
We could cook more vegetables.

Ihr solltet **regelmäßig Karate machen.**
You should do karate regularly.

Sie sollten **fettes Essen vermeiden.**
They should avoid fatty foods.

Sie könnten **etwas zunehmen.**
You could put on a little weight.

❓ Test Yourself

What do these mean in English?
1. **Ich bin übergewichtig und ein Stubenhocker.**
2. **Ich bin eine Naschkatze und esse gern Bonbons.**

How do you say these in German?
3. My brain hurts.
4. I have a sore throat.

⭐ Stretch Yourself

1. Say or write in English: '**Um in Form zu bleiben, sollte man jeden Tag zum Training gehen, weil es gesund ist.**'
2. Say or write in German: 'I have broken my left arm and my right foot and it hurts!'

Smoking, Alcohol, Drugs

Smoking

Rauchst du?	Do you smoke?
Ich rauche (nicht).	I (don't) smoke.
Ich habe nie geraucht.	I have never smoked.
Ich habe damit aufgehört.	I have given up.

Seit wann rauchst du?
How long have you been smoking for?

Ich rauche seit zwei Jahren. Ich bin 19 Jahre alt.
I have been smoking for two years. I'm 19 years old.

Warum raucht man?
Why do people smoke?

Ich rauche (nie), weil...	I (never) smoke, because...
meine Freunde das machen.	my friends do it.
ich Diät halte.	I'm on a diet.
das teuer / tödlich / ungesund / ekelhaft ist.	it is expensive / deadly / unhealthy / disgusting.
das so stinkt.	it really stinks.
ich süchtig bin.	I am addicted.

Build Your Skills: Opinions Using 'Dass'

It is important that you give lots of opinions and use a selection of complex grammar in your work. Combine an opinion using **, dass**, or **, weil** or **, wenn**, etc. to give more detail and add complexity. Remember to kick the first verb to the end of the sentence.

Ich denke, dass **Rauchen eine Geldverschwendung** ist.
I think that smoking is a waste of money.

Ich glaube, dass **Rauchen ekelhaft** ist, weil **Zigaretten soviel Teer** enthalten.
I believe that smoking is disgusting, because cigarettes contain so much tar.

Ich weiß, dass **viele Leute an Lungenkrebs** sterben, weil **mein Opa daran gestorben** ist.
I know that many people die of lung cancer, because my granddad died of it.

Ich finde, dass **die Haare und Kleidung nach Zigaretten** stinken, wenn **man immer** raucht.
I find that your hair and clothes stink of cigarettes when you always smoke.

Ich mache mir Sorgen, dass **ich ein Alkoholproblem** habe, weil **ich immer mehr** trinke.
I am worried that I have an alcohol problem, because I'm drinking more and more.

Alcohol

Trinkst du Alkohol?
Do you drink alcohol?

Ich habe nie Alkohol probiert.
I have never tried alcohol.

Mit fünfzehn Jahren habe ich mein erstes Bier getrunken.
I drank my first beer at the age of 15.

Seit drei Jahren trinke ich viel Wein.
I have been drinking a lot of wine for three years.

Jedes Wochenende ist mein Vater betrunken.
Every weekend my father is drunk.

Er hat ein Alkoholproblem.
He has an alcohol problem.

Jamie ist Alkoholiker.
Jamie is an alcoholic.

Seine Familie ist daran Schuld.
It's his family's fault.

Mein Vater hat mir ein Glas Apfelwein gegeben.
My father gave me a glass of cider.

Drugs

Warum nimmt man Drogen?
Why do people take drugs?

Man sollte nie Drogen nehmen.
You should never take drugs.

Viele Jugendliche greifen zu Drogen, weil sie denken, dass sie cool sind.
Many people turn to drugs, because they think that they are cool.

Neben den illegalen Drogen wie Cannabis / Heroin / Kokain, gibt es auch legale Drogen wie Koffein / Schlankheitstabletten.
Besides illegal drugs like cannabis / heroin / cocaine, there are also legal drugs like caffeine / slimming pills.

Was denkst du über Drogen?
What do you think about drugs?

Ich bin total gegen Drogennehmen.
I'm totally against taking drugs.

Für mich ist Drogenkonsum das größte Problem für Jugendliche.
I think that drug consumption is the biggest youth problem.

Es ist ziemlich schwierig, Drogen aufzugeben.
It is quite difficult to give up drugs.

Man soll Drogen auf jeden Fall vermeiden.
You should avoid drugs at all costs.

Ich habe Angst, dass mein Bruder mit Drogen anfangen wird.
I'm afraid that my brother will start with drugs.

Leisure and Lifestyle

Build Your Skills: The Importance of 'Zu'

Some expressions require the word **zu** (to) in the sentence (see also page 16). The **zu** clause is separated from the main verb by a comma with the infinitive at the end. You can also use **zu** when saying what is important to you:

Was ist dir wichtig?	What is important to you?
Es ist mir (sehr) wichtig,...	It is (very) important to me...
in der Klasse beliebt zu **sein.**	to be popular in the class.
meine Eltern nicht zu **enttäuschen.**	not to disappoint my parents.
die Prüfungen zu **bestehen.**	to pass the exams.

✓ Maximise Your Marks

When using subordinating conjunctions, like **weil**, always make sure you have included the verb at the end of the sentence. It is a common mistake to forget the verb completely!

❓ Test Yourself

What do these mean in English?
1. **Es ist ziemlich schwierig, Kokain aufzugeben.**
2. **Mit 18 Jahren habe ich mein erstes Bier getrunken.**

How do you say these in German?
3. I have never smoked because it is deadly.
4. It's my father's fault.

⭐ Stretch Yourself

1. Say or write in English: '**Ich weiß, dass mein Onkel Alkoholiker ist, aber man sollte Wodka auf jeden Fall vermeiden, weil das ungesund ist.**'
2. Say or write in German: 'It is very important to me to pass my exams.'

Practice Questions

 Complete these exam-style questions to test your skills and understanding. Check your answers on pages 92–93. You may wish to answer these questions on a separate piece of paper.

Reading

1 Four students are writing about free time and technology. Read the passages below and answer the questions that follow.

Normalerweise höre ich gern Popmusik. Ich kaufe entweder CDs oder ich lade Musik aus dem Internet herunter. Gestern bin ich ins Kino gegangen und ich habe einen Liebesfilm gesehen.	Günther
Mein Handy ist mein Leben. Mit dem Handy lese ich Zeitungen, surfe ich im Internet, besuche ich Chatrooms und fotografiere ich viel, aber ich kann damit nicht fernsehen.	Silke
Ich sehe mir gern Zeichentrickfilme auf dem PC an und ich höre immer Musik auf meinem Handy. Morgen werde ich endlich einen neuen MP3-Spieler kaufen. Das wird toll!	Serdar
Viele junge Leute verbringen zu viel Zeit im Internet. Sie besuchen oft Chatrooms und haben Freunde in aller Welt. Das finde ich gefährlich und unsicher.	Daniela

a) Who reads newspapers? .... (1)

b) Who will do some shopping tomorrow? .... (1)

c) Who talks about the dangers of the web? .... (1)

d) Who downloads pop music? .... (1)

e) Who likes films? .... (2)

f) Who would hate social networking sites? .... (1)

2 Shamir is talking about a wedding he attended in Germany. Read the text and answer the questions.

Ich liege zur Zeit im Bett und höre Musik – ich bin so müde! Gestern war ich auf einer Hochzeit in München. Es war einmalig! Zuerst haben wir Pfirsiche für die Obsttorte vom Markt gekauft, dann haben wir uns schick angezogen und viel getanzt. Ich habe einen Anzug aus Leder getragen! Zum Abschluss hatte mein Onkel ein großes Feuerwerk vorbereitet. Es war echt laut. Ich denke, dass ich meinen siebzehnten Geburtstag in Deutschland feiern werde. Wir werden ein Grillfest machen und ich möchte eine Tätowierung als Geschenk bekommen, weil das cool aussehen würde.

a) What is Shamir doing at the moment?

....

.... (2)

b) How is he feeling?

....

.... (1)

c) What did he buy from the market and why?

.... (2)

d) What did Shamir wear?

.... (1)

e) What had his uncle arranged and how was it?

.... (2)

f) What three things will he do for his 17th birthday?

.... (3)

Speaking

3 You are new in town and want to record a short video to post on the 'FreundeFinden' website. Prepare to discuss the following points in German in full sentences. Include opinions and develop your answers where possible. When you are ready, record yourself on your phone.

a) Describe what you do in your free time and why.

....

b) Say what you use computers for and why.

....

c) Describe an event you went to in the past.

....

d) Describe a film you will see in the future.

.... (10)

Writing

4 You are writing a short essay on 'healthy living' to enter into the Hamburg short essay competition. The prize is a trip to the island of Sylt. You need to develop each point and give lots of opinions.

- Describe what you do to keep fit and why.
- Describe what you usually eat and drink and say if it's healthy.
- Discuss your views on smoking, alcohol and drugs.

....

....

....

....

....

....

.... (15)

How well did you do?

| 0–10 | Try again | 11–20 | Getting there | 21–32 | Good work | 33–43 | Excellent! |

Holiday Destinations

Countries

Afrika	Africa	**Indien**	India	**die Vereinigten Staaten****	USA
Amerika	America	**Irland**	Ireland	**Wales**	Wales
Asien	Asia	**Italien**	Italy		
Australien	Australia	**Japan**	Japan		
Belgien	Belgium	**die Niederlande****	Netherlands		
China	China	**Österreich**	Austria		
Dänemark	Denmark	**Pakistan**	Pakistan		
Deutschland	Germany	**Polen**	Poland		
England	England	**Russland**	Russia		
Europa	Europe	**Schottland**	Scotland		
Frankreich	France	**die Schweiz***	Switzerland		
Griechenland	Greece	**Spanien**	Spain		
Großbritannien	Great Britain	**die Türkei***	Turkey	* feminine ** plural	

Build Your Skills: To and In

Most countries in German are neuter. For neuter and masculine countries use **nach** (to) to say *to* a country and **in** (in) for *in* a country:

- **Ich fahre** nach **Brasilien.** I am going *to* Brazil.
- **Ich wohne** in **Mexiko.** I live *in* Mexico.

For feminine countries you need to use **in die** for 'to' and **in der** for 'in':

- **Wir fahren** in die **Türkei.**
  We're going *to* Turkey.

- **Sie wohnt** in der **Schweiz.**
  She lives *in* Switzerland.

For plural countries you use **in die** for 'to' and **in den** for 'in':

- **Ich fliege** in die **Niederlande.**
  I'm flying *to* the Netherlands.
- **Sie wohnen** in den **Vereinigten Staaten.**
  They live *in* the USA.

Nationalities / Adjectives

Nationality words change if the subject is feminine or plural:

Ich bin Engländer(in).
I'm (an) English (woman).

When describing an item using a nationality adjective, you need to include the correct ending. This adjective does *not* start with a capital letter in German:

- **Ich habe ein englisches Auto / einen irischen Pass.**
  I have an English car / an Irish passport.

Afrikaner(in) / afrikanisch	African
Amerikaner(in) / amerikanisch	American
Belgier(in) / belgisch	Belgian
Engländer(in) / englisch	English
Inder(in) / indisch	Indian
Italiener(in) / italienisch	Italian
Japaner(in) / japanisch	Japanese
Niederländer(in) / niederländisch	Dutch
Österreicher(in) / österreichisch	Austrian
Spanier(in) / spanisch	Spanish
Brite / Britin / britisch	British
Deutsche(r) / deutsch	German
Franzose / Französin / französisch	French
Ire / Irin / irisch	Irish
Schotte / Schottin / schottisch	Scottish
Waliser / Waliserin / walisisch	Welsh

Holiday Destinations

an der Küste	on the coast
auf dem Land	in the country
im Gebirge	in the mountains
in einer Stadt	in a city
bei meiner Oma	at my grandma's

Wo fährst du gern hin?
Where do you like going?

Ich fahre (nicht) gern nach Italien.
I (don't) like going to Italy.

Ich bleibe lieber zu Hause.
I prefer to stay at home.

Am liebsten fliege ich in die Türkei.
I like flying to Turkey best of all.

Mit wem fährst du in Urlaub?
Who are you going on holiday with?

Ich fahre oft (mit meiner Familie) in Urlaub.
I often go on holiday (with my family).

meistens alleine	mostly on my own
mit Freunden	with friends

Wie findest du die Ferien?
What do you think of the holidays?

Die Ferien sind entspannend / erholsam / schön.
The holidays are relaxing / restful / lovely.

Ich bin nach Polen gefahren.
I went to Poland.

Wir sind in die Vereinigten Staaten geflogen.
We flew to the United States.

Build Your Skills: Who's Who

There are four words for 'who' in German: **wer**, **wen**, **wessen**, **wem**. The correct one to use depends on the case or on a preceding preposition:

Nominative	**wer**	who
Accusative	**wen**	who(m)
Genitive	**wessen**	whose
Dative	**wem**	(to) whom

Mit wem **fliegst du?**
With whom are you flying?

✓ Maximise Your Marks

For the higher grades, the examiner wants to see sentences full of information. See how you can make this sentence more interesting:

- **Ich bin nach Wien gefahren.**
  I went to Vienna.

Add a time word:

- **Ich bin** in den Ferien **nach Wien gefahren.**
  I went to Vienna in the holidays.

Add details about who you went with:

- **Ich bin in den Ferien** mit meinen Eltern **nach Wien gefahren.**
  I went to Vienna in the holidays with my parents.

Add details about how you got there:

- **Ich bin in den Ferien mit meinen Eltern** mit dem Zug **nach Wien gefahren.**
  I went to Vienna in the holidays with my parents by train.

Add interesting adjectives to your sentences:

- **Ich bin in den** Oster**ferien mit meinen** strengen **Eltern mit dem** glänzenden **ICE Zug nach Wien gefahren.**
  I went to Vienna in the Easter holidays with my strict parents on the shiny ICE train.

❓ Test Yourself

What do these mean in English?

1. **Am liebsten fliegen wir nach Spanien.**
2. **Ich bin Amerikanerin, aber ich habe einen deutschen Pass.**

How do you say these in German?

3. I am Japanese and I like going to Asia.
4. I often go on holiday with friends.

⭐ Stretch Yourself

1. Say or write in English: '**Ich weiß, mit wem ich in die Schweiz geflogen bin: Mit meiner alten Tante**.'
2. Say or write in German: 'I went to Greece with friends last year.'

Travel and Getting Around

Directions

Wie komme ich am besten...?	What's the best way to get...?
zum Museum	to the museum
zum Parkplatz	to the car park
zum Geldautomaten	to the cash machine
zum Bahnhof	to the railway station
zur Schule	to the school

Ist hier eine Bank in der Nähe?
Is there a bank near here?

Wo ist die nächste Polizeiwache?
Where is the nearest police station?

An der Kreuzung...	At the crossroads...
An der Ampel...	At the traffic lights...
biegen Sie rechts / links ab	turn right / left
gehen Sie geradeaus weiter	go straight on
fahren Sie bis zum Kreisverkehr	drive to the roundabout
fahren Sie die Straße entlang	drive along the road

Transport

Ich bin... gefahren.	I went...
mit dem Auto	by car
mit dem Bus	by bus
mit dem Flugzeug	by plane
mit dem Zug	by train
mit dem (Kreuzfahrt) Schiff	by (cruise) ship
mit dem (Fahr)Rad	by bike
mit dem Hubschrauber	by helicopter
mit der U-Bahn	by underground / tube
mit der Straßenbahn	by tram
mit der Fähre	by ferry

Ich bin zu Fuß gegangen.   I went on foot.

The Imperative

To give instructions or directions you need to use the imperative.

If you are speaking to a person whom you address as **du**, you take the **du** form of a verb and chop off the **–st** and omit the **du**:

du gehst = you go ➡ **Geh...!** = Go...!

If you are speaking to people whom you address as **ihr**, you take the **ihr** form of a verb and omit the **ihr**:

ihr geht = you go (plural) ➡ **Geht...!** = Go...!

If you are speaking to people whom you address as **Sie**, you invert the verb and the word **Sie**:

Sie gehen = you go (formal) ➡ **Gehen Sie...!** = Go...!

To tell someone *not* to do something you insert the word **nicht** after the instructions above:

Geh nicht...! Don't go...!

With separable verbs, the prefix goes to the end of the instruction:

Komm sicher an! Arrive safely!

Travelling Verbs

fahren**	to go / to travel / to drive
fliegen**	to fly
gehen**	to go
*abfahren** / *abfliegen**	to depart
*ankommen**	to arrive
*aussteigen**	to get off / to alight
*einsteigen**	to get on
Rad fahren	to cycle
*umsteigen**	to change trains
*abholen	to pick up / to fetch
reisen	to travel
überholen	to overtake
starten	to take off (plane)
landen	to land (plane)
vermieten	to rent / to hire
verlassen	to leave

* separable verb
** verb taking **sein** in the perfect tense

Build Your Skills: The Perfect Tense and Travel

On page 34 you reviewed the perfect tense. You saw that verbs which indicate motion to or away from an object or place take the auxiliary verb **sein** (to be) and a past participle:

- **Ich bin mit dem Bus gefahren.**
  I went by bus.

If the verb is separable, the **ge–** is sandwiched between the separable bit and the rest of the past participle:

- **Wir sind pünktlich abgefahren.**
  We departed on time.

Most verbs take **haben** (to have) as their auxiliary verb. If the verb is separable, the same rule as above applies with the past participle:

- **Mein Opa hat mich mit dem Mofa abgeholt.**
  My grandad fetched me on the moped.

Describing a Recent Journey

der Flug	the flight
die Autofahrt	the car journey
die Kreuzfahrt	the cruise
die Reise	the trip

Wir haben einen Urlaub in Italien gebucht.
We booked a holiday in Italy.

Wir sind um acht Uhr (mit der U-Bahn) zum Flughafen gefahren.
We went to the airport at eight o'clock (by tube).

Wir sind dort um neun Uhr angekommen.
We arrived there at nine o'clock.

Wir sind um elf Uhr mit dem Flugzeug von London abgeflogen.
We departed from London at 11 o'clock by plane.

Unterwegs...	On the way...
haben wir viel geplaudert	we chatted a lot
haben wir uns verirrt	we got lost
war uns / mir übel	we / I felt sick

Meiner Meinung nach war der Flug...	In my opinion the flight was...
angenehm	pleasant
ermüdend	tiring
stressig	stressful
langsam ≠ schnell	slow ≠ fast

✓ Maximise Your Marks

Take care when talking about different modes of transport. In English we usually say 'by' a means of transport (by bus, by car, etc.) but in German this is usually 'with the': **mit dem Bus** (by bus), **mit dem Auto** (by car), etc.

But **zu Fuß** for 'on foot'.

❓ Test Yourself

What do these mean in English?
1. **Wir sind mit der Fähre gefahren.**
2. **Meiner Meinung nach war die Reise ermüdend.**

How do you say these in German?
3. What's the best way to get to the station?
4. At the traffic lights turn right! (formal **Sie**)

⭐ Stretch Yourself

1. Say or write in English: '**Mein Opa ist mit dem Hubschrauber nach Deutschland geflogen. Er ist schneller als ich angekommen.**'
2. Say or write in German: 'Change trains quickly!' (**Sie**)

Accommodation and Problems

Holiday Accommodation

Wo hast du übernachtet?
Where did you stay?

Ich habe... übernachtet.	I stayed...
im Hotel	in a hotel
im Gasthaus	in a guesthouse
in einer Jugendherberge	in a youth hostel
auf einem Campingplatz	on a campsite
im Zelt	in a tent
im Wohnwagen	in a caravan
im Freien	in the open air
zu Hause	at home
bei Freunden	at friends'

Wie lange hast du dort verbracht?
How long did you stay there?

Wir haben... dort verbracht.	We stayed there for...
eine Woche	a week
eine Nacht / zwei Nächte	one night / two nights
ein (langes) Wochenende	a (long) weekend
zehn Tage	10 days
zwei Wochen	a fortnight (two weeks)

Facilities

Ich möchte bitte... reservieren.	I would like to reserve..., please.
ein Doppelzimmer	a double room
ein Einzelzimmer	a single room
ein Mehrbettzimmer	a family room
ein Zimmer	a room
im Erdgeschoss	on the ground floor
im ersten Stock / auf der ersten Etage	on the first floor
mit Blick auf (+ acc.)...	with a view of...

die Unterkunft	accommodation
die Halbpension	half board
die Vollpension	full board
der Balkon	balcony
die Klimaanlage	air conditioning
der Spiegel	mirror
die Dusche	shower
die Seife	soap
das Bad	bath
das Badezimmer	bathroom
das Shampoo	shampoo
das Handtuch	towel
das Toilettenpapier	toilet paper
die Bettwäsche	bedlinen
das Doppelbett	double bed
das Kopfkissen	pillow

Build Your Skills: Imperfect Tense (Simple Past)

The imperfect tense, or simple past as it is also known, is used to describe events in the past.

It is regularly formed with the verb **sein** to say 'was' / 'were' and **haben** to say 'had':

ich war	I was
du warst	you were
er / sie / es war	he / she / it was
wir waren	we were
ihr wart	you were
sie waren	they were
Sie waren	you were (formal)

ich hatte	I had
du hattest	you had
er / sie / es hatte	he / she / it had
wir hatten	we had
ihr hattet	you had
sie hatten	they had
Sie hatten	you had (formal)

The following is also common:

Es gab...   There was / were...

With other verbs the imperfect can be translated as 'I did', 'I was doing' or 'I used to do'. It is usually used in writing to describe a past event.

Build Your Skills: Imperfect Tense (Simple Past) (cont.)

To form the imperfect tense of *regular* verbs, find the stem of the verb and add the following endings:

ich spielte	I played, was playing
du kauftest	you bought, were buying
er / sie / es tanzte	he / she / it danced, was dancing
wir übernachteten	we stayed, were staying
ihr zeltetet	you camped, were camping
sie machten	they made, were making
Sie putzten	you cleaned, were cleaning

To form the imperfect tense of *irregular* verbs, find the stem of the verb in the back of a dictionary or textbook and add these endings to the stem given:

ich fuhr	I travelled, was travelling
du gingst	you went, were going
er / sie / es aß	he / she / it ate, was eating
wir schliefen	we slept, were sleeping
ihr trankt	you drank, were drinking
sie blieben	they stayed, were staying
Sie sangen	you sang, were singing

Problems on Holiday

Ich habe... verloren.	I've lost...
Man hat mir... gestohlen.	I've had... stolen.
die Brieftasche	wallet
den Fotoapparat	camera
den Reisepass	passport
den Schlüssel	key

Leider gab es...	Unfortunately, there was / were...
einen Verkehrsunfall	a road accident
einen Stau	a traffic jam
keine Badetücher / Handtücher im Badezimmer	no bath towels / (hand)towels in the bathroom
kein Klopapier	no toilet paper

Das Hotel / Restaurant / Zimmer / Essen war / hatte...
The hotel / restaurant / room / food was / had...

ekelhaft ≠ lecker / köstlich	disgusting ≠ delicious
alt ≠ neu	old ≠ new
muffig ≠ frisch	musty ≠ fresh
teuer ≠ preiswert	expensive ≠ good value
kalt ≠ heiß	cold ≠ hot
hart ≠ weich	hard ≠ soft
keine Minibar / Vorhänge	no minibar / curtains
kein sauberes Besteck	no clean cutlery
keinen Aufzug / Empfang	no lift / reception

Das Fernsehgerät im Zimmer funktionierte nicht.
The TV in the room was not working.

Die Angestellten / Kellner waren / hatten...
The staff / waiters were / had...

faul ≠ hilfsbereit	lazy ≠ helpful
(un)aufmerksam	(in)attentive
unhöflich ≠ höflich	impolite ≠ polite
unfreundlich ≠ freundlich	unfriendly ≠ friendly
absolut keine Ahnung	absolutely no idea
schlechte Manieren	bad manners

💡 Boost Your Memory

Learning words in pairs is a good way to increase your vocabulary. Why not learn opposites like **schmutzig ≠ sauber** (dirty ≠ clean) or synonyms like **lecker = köstlich** (delicious).

❓ Test Yourself

What do these mean in English?

1. **Wir haben drei Nächte dort verbracht.**
2. **Das Zimmer hatte keinen Balkon.**

How do you say these in German?

3. I stayed in a caravan.
4. I'd like to reserve a family room, please.

⭐ Stretch Yourself

1. Say or write in English: '**Das Zimmer im vierten Stock hatte alte Bettwäsche und die Klimaanlage funktionierte nicht.**'
2. Say or write in German: 'I was staying in a youth hostel, but unfortunately there were no soft towels.'

Holiday Activities

Activities

Andenken kaufen	to buy souvenirs
angeln gehen	to go fishing
den Freizeitpark besuchen	to visit the theme park
die Museen besuchen	to visit the museums
*fernsehen	to watch TV
ein Auto / Mofa mieten	to rent a car / moped
ein gutes Buch lesen	to read a good book
auf Safari gehen	to go on safari
sich eine Show ansehen	to watch a show
einen Stadtbummel machen	to go for a walk around town
eine Stadttour machen	to go on a city tour
(in den Bergen) wandern gehen	to go hiking (in the mountains)
in die Disko gehen	to go to the disco
ins Restaurant gehen	to go to a restaurant
ins Theater gehen	to go to the theatre
Kamelreiten gehen	to ride a camel
Minigolf spielen	to play crazy golf
mit den Einheimischen flirten	to flirt with the locals
Musik am Strand hören	to listen to music on the beach
neue Leute / Kulturen *kennenlernen	to get to know new people / cultures
picknicken	to go on a picnic
Sandburgen bauen	to build sandcastles
schwimmen gehen	to go swimming
sich die Sehenswürdigkeiten *anschauen	to go sightseeing
sich sonnen	to lounge in the sun
skifahren gehen	to go skiing
*sonnenbaden	to sunbathe
windsurfen lernen	to learn to windsurf
Volleyball spielen	to play volleyball

* separable verb

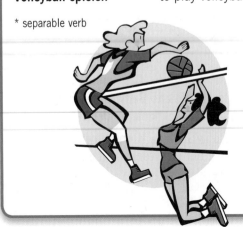

Build Your Skills: Talking About Time

Expressions of time add interest to your written and spoken work.

These time words can be used when talking about the past:

letztes Jahr	last year
letzte Woche	last year
am Sonntagabend	Sunday evening
gestern	yesterday
letzten Sommer	last summer
früher	in the past
vor zwei / drei Jahren	two / three years ago
in den Sommerferien	in the summer holidays

When starting with a time word, the verb needs to be in second place. This adds complexity to your sentence:

1	2	3	
Letzten Winter	habe	ich	Minigolf gespielt.
Last winter I played crazy golf.			

Sequencers are used in the same way as time words. These sequencers can be used to tell a story:

erstens	first of all
zweitens	second(ly)
am ersten Tag	on the first day
am nächsten / letzten Tag	the next / last day
danach	afterwards
dann	then
zum Schluss	at the end
am Ende der Ferien	at the end of the holidays
alles in allem	all in all

Use a variety of tenses in your work for higher marks. When talking about what you did in your holidays, include a future or conditional tense and say what you will or would do in the future:

Letztes Jahr bin ich auf Safari gegangen. Nächstes Jahr werde ich Kamelreiten gehen.

Last year I went on safari. Next year I will go camel riding.

My Last Holiday

Was hast du in den Ferien gemacht?
What did you do in the holidays?

Vor zwei Jahren sind wir nach Spanien gefahren.
Two years ago we went to Spain.

Wir haben im Hotel Fiesta übernachtet.
We stayed at Hotel Fiesta.

Ich habe jeden Tag Eis gegessen.
I ate ice cream every day.

Am ersten Tag hat sich meine Schwester eine Show angesehen.
On the first day my sister saw a show.

Am nächsten Tag haben wir uns am Strand gesonnt.
The next day we sunbathed on the beach.

Danach haben meine Eltern die Museen besucht.
Afterwards my parents visited the museums.

Ich habe große Sandburgen gebaut, während meine Schwester Musik hörte.
I made big sandcastles, while my sister was listening to music.

Am letzten Tag ist mein Vater angeln gegangen.
On the last day my dad went fishing.

Wir sind in die Stadt gegangen und haben kitschige Andenken gekauft.
We went into town and bought tacky souvenirs.

Alles in allem haben wir viel Spaß gehabt.
All in all we had a lot of fun.

Ich möchte wieder in Spanien urlauben.
I would like to have another holiday in Spain.

My Ideal Holiday

Vary your tenses and include future wishes in your work about holidays.

Was sind deine idealen Ferien?
What are your ideal holidays?

Ich möchte nach Amerika fahren.
I would like to travel to America.

Ich will in den Kaufhäusern von New York einkaufen gehen.
I want to go shopping in the department stores in New York.

Wenn ich das Geld hätte, würde ich erster Klasse fliegen.
If I had the money, I would fly first class.

Ich würde in einem Luxushotel übernachten.
I would stay in a luxury hotel.

Es wird / würde viel Spaß machen.
It will / would be a lot of fun.

Wir wollen auf Safari in Afrika gehen.
We want to go on (a) safari in Africa.

✓ Maximise Your Marks

Talking about the past using both the imperfect and the perfect tense would count as two tenses and boost your grade. Try combining them in your work, together with other tenses.

❓ Test Yourself

What do these mean in English?
1. Ich habe ein Mofa gemietet.
2. Ich will Musik am Strand hören.

How do you say these in German?
3. Three years ago we went to Italy.
4. I'd like to go skiing.

⭐ Stretch Yourself

1. Say or write in English: '**Am ersten Tag würde ich mir die Sehenswürdigkeiten anschauen und am letzten Tag will ich angeln lernen.**'
2. Say or write in German: 'Yesterday we sunbathed and afterwards we flirted with the locals.'

Life in Other Countries

Holidays and Travel

German-speaking Locations

The German language is not spoken only in Germany. It is also an official language of Austria, Switzerland, Liechtenstein and Luxembourg.

Deutschland	Germany
Österreich	Austria
die Schweiz	Switzerland
Liechtenstein	Liechtenstein
Luxemburg	Luxembourg
die Deutschen	the Germans
die Österreicher	the Austrians
die Schweizer	the Swiss
die Liechtensteiner	the Liechtensteiners
die Luxemburger	the Luxembourgers

Deutsch wird von ungefähr 126 Millionen Bürgern gesprochen.
German is spoken by around 126 million citizens.

Die Schweizer sprechen Schweizerdeutsch.
The Swiss speak Swiss German.

Es gibt viele Dialekte.
There are many dialects.

Deutsch ist die meistgesprochene Sprache innerhalb der Europäischen Union.
German is the most widely spoken language in the European Union.

✓ Maximise Your Marks

When discussing what languages you speak, you could develop your answer further by including a fact about where German is spoken and how many people speak it.

Including statistics in your work is an excellent way to prepare for A-level German.

Towns, Cities and Regions

The names of German-speaking towns, cities and regions may appear in your reading and listening tests. Some of these towns, cities and regions are spelt differently in German:

Die Hauptstadt von Deutschland ist Berlin.
The capital of Germany is Berlin.

Wien	Vienna (Austria)
Bern	Berne (Switzerland)
Luxemburg	Luxembourg City
Köln	Cologne (Germany)
München	Munich (Germany)
Nürnberg	Nuremberg (Germany)
Genf	Geneva (Switzerland)
Zürich	Zurich (Switzerland)

Deutschland ist eine Bundesrepublik.
Germany is a Federal Republic.

Es gibt sechzehn Bundesländer.
There are 16 Federal States.

Bayern	Bavaria
Thüringen	Thuringia
Sachsen	Saxony

Deutschland hat ungefähr 82 Millionen Einwohner.
Germany has around 82 million inhabitants.

Build Your Skills: Prepositions

Prepositions tell us where things are. Some prepositions are followed by the accusative.

für (for), **u**m (round / at), **d**urch (through), **g**egen (against), **e**ntlang (along), **b**is (until), **o**hne (without), **w**ider (against)

Remember: fudge bow – the first letter of each accusative preposition!

Some prepositions are followed by the dative if no movement is involved:

an (to / at), **auf** (on), **hinter** (behind), **in** (in), **neben** (next to), **über** (over), **unter** (under), **vor** (against), **zwischen** (between)

Landscape

The names of mountain ranges, rivers, lakes and seas may also appear in your reading and listening tests.

Hamburg liegt an der Elbe.
Hamburg is on the river Elbe.

der Fluss	river
der Rhein	Rhine
die Donau	Danube
die Mosel	Moselle

Man kann... besuchen.	You can visit...
die Alpen	the Alps
den Bodensee	Lake Constance
die Nordsee	the North Sea
die Ostsee	the Baltic Sea
den Schwarzwald	the Black Forest
das Brandenburger Tor	the Brandenburg Gate
den Kölner Dom	Cologne Cathedral
den Reichstag	the Reichstag (German parliament)

Culture

There are many customs and traditions in German-speaking countries.

die Gewohnheit	habit
die Lederhose	leather trousers
das Dirndlkleid	dirndl dress
jodeln	to yodel
das Radler / Alsterwasser	shandy
die Schwarzwälder Kirschtorte	Black Forest gateau

die Sachertorte	Sacher cake
der Apfelstrudel	apple strudel
kein Tempolimit auf der Autobahn	no speed limit on the motorway
Schlange stehen	to form a queue

Es wird gesagt, dass die Deutschen sehr ernst / pünktlich / organisiert sind.
It is said that the Germans are very serious / punctual / organised.

Schools in Germany

The German school system is different to the one in the UK. They have five main types of school, which you need to be aware of as they may appear in your reading or listening papers.

das Gymnasium – an academic school for the most academic pupils. Prepares them for **das Abitur** (A-levels)

die Realschule – similar to a secondary modern school, offering a wide range of subjects from age 10 to 16

die Hauptschule – lower secondary school with a more vocational and practical focus

die Gesamtschule – like a comprehensive school in the UK. Combines all of the schools above in one

die Oberstufe – sixth form, normally part of a Gymnasium school

Deutsche Schüler tragen keine Uniform.
German students don't wear a uniform.

Die Schule beginnt um halb acht und endet um halb zwei.
School begins at half past seven and ends at half past one.

Am Nachmittag nehmen viele deutsche Schüler an AGs teil.
In the afternoon many German pupils go to after-school clubs.

Im Gymnasium macht man das Abitur.
At the Gymnasium school you do the Abitur (A-levels).

Holidays and Travel

? Test Yourself

Unjumble the letters to find a German word:
1 nearBy
2 retrocheatS
3 sluGmachetes
4 Beenosed

★ Stretch Yourself

1 Say or write in English: '**Ich glaube, dass die deutsche Sprache von ungefähr 126 Millionen Bürgern gesprochen wird.**'
2 Say or write in German: 'You can visit Cologne Cathedral.'

Practice Questions

 Complete these exam-style questions to test your skills and understanding. Check your answers on pages 93–94. You may wish to answer these questions on a separate piece of paper.

Reading

1 Fill in the gaps using six of the seven words below:

Englisch	gefahren	Engländer	Millionen	bin	sind	Jugendherberge

> Guten Tag! Ich heiße Robert und ich bin (a) .... (1). Ich kann (b) .... (1) und
>
> ein bisschen Deutsch. Letztes Jahr sind wir nach Wien (c) .... (1). Das ist die
>
> Hauptstadt von Österreich, das ungefähr 8,5 (d) .... (1) Einwohner hat. Dort haben wir in
>
> einer (e) .... (1) übernachtet. Es war sehr alt aber gemütlich. Wir haben viel gemacht.
>
> Ich (f) .... (1) zum ersten Mal Skilaufen gegangen. Das war total unglaublich!

2 Read the email below from Lawrence describing a past holiday. Answer the questions in English.

> Vor vier Jahren bin ich mit dem Auto in die deutschen Alpen gefahren, um snowboarden zu gehen. Ich habe zehn schöne Tage mit meiner Familie im Hotel Mexx verbracht. Die Reise war wirklich ermüdend, weil sie zwanzig Stunden dauerte, aber das Hotel war ganz modern. Am zweiten Tag sind wir nach München gefahren und haben uns die Sehenswürdigkeiten angeschaut. Die Stadt ist sehr schön. In den nächsten Ferien möchte ich nicht in Deutschland urlauben, sondern ich würde gern Österreich sehen.

a) Where did Lawrence go and why?

.... (2)

b) How long did he stay and who with?

.... (2)

c) How did he get there?

.... (1)

d) What was his opinion of the journey and why?

.... (2)

e) Where did he stay and what was it like?

.... (2)

f) What did he do on the second day?

....

.... (2)

g) Where would he like to go on holiday next?

.... (1)

Speaking

3 You are talking to your German friend on the phone about your recent holiday. Discuss the following points in German in full sentences. Give opinions and develop your answers when possible. When you are ready, record yourself on your phone.

a) Describe where you went and how you got there.

b) Say where you stayed and what you thought of it.

c) Say what you did during your visit and give opinions.

d) Say where you would like to go next year and what you will do.

(10)

Writing

4 You love complaining and recently experienced the *worst* holiday ever. Everything that could have gone wrong, did go wrong. Write an email to your German friend explaining everything. Give opinions! Cover the following points:

- Describe the nightmare journey.
- Describe the horrible accommodation.
- Where would you go on holiday if you had the money?

(15)

5 You are writing a short essay about favourite holiday destinations and Germany as a holiday location. You need to develop each of the following points and give lots of opinions. You may also need to use your imagination!

- State your nationality and what countries you have visited.
- Explain where you do and do not like to go on holiday and why.
- Describe a recent trip to Germany and give facts about the country. Would you return?

(15)

How well did you do?

| 0–13 | Try again | 14–27 | Getting there | 28–42 | Good work | 43–58 | Excellent! |

The Environment

Doing My Bit

Bist du umweltfreundlich?
Are you environmentally friendly?

Ich bin (ziemlich) umweltfreundlich.
I am (quite) environmentally friendly.

Was machst du, um die Umwelt zu schützen?
What do you do to protect the environment?

Ich trenne den Müll.
I separate the rubbish.

Ich drehe den Hahn zu, während ich mir die Zähne putzte.
I turn off the tap while I'm cleaning my teeth.

Ich recycele Altglas und Altpapier.
I recycle used glass and paper.

Ich kompostiere den Abfall.
I compost rubbish.

Ich nehme immer eine Öko-Tasche mit.
I always use an eco-friendly shopping bag.

Ich kaufe umweltfreundliche Produkte.
I buy environmentally friendly products.

Ich fahre mit öffentlichen Verkehrsmitteln.
I use public transport.

Wir sind aufmerksam, wenn wir einkaufen gehen.
We pay attention when we go shopping.

Ich dusche, anstatt ein Bad zu nehmen.
I take a shower instead of taking a bath.

Ich fahre mit dem Rad.
I go by bike.

Build Your Skills: What Else Could We Do?

To extend a response about what you do to help the environment, use modal verbs in the conditional mood to describe what you should or could do to help. This adds complexity and an additional tense to your work, as well as developing your answer further. Here are some examples of how you can use modal verbs in this way:

Man könnte...	You could...
Man sollte...	You should...
Man müsste...	You would have to...
Man dürfte...	You might...

die Zimmer sparsam heizen	heat your rooms economically
keine Plastiktüte benutzen	not use plastic bags
Geräte immer ausschalten	always turn off electric appliances
aufhören, Wasser zu verschwenden	stop wasting water
verspechen, in Zukunft noch mehr zu tun	promise to do even more in the future
den CO₂-Fußabdruck reduzieren	reduce your carbon footprint

Man könnte die Umwelt wirklich beeinflussen, wenn man beim Einkaufen global denken würde.
We could really have an effect on the environment, if we were to think globally when we shop.

Expressing Opinions

Ist dir Umweltschutz wichtig?
Is environmental protection important to you?

Ja, ich halte Umweltschutz für total wichtig.
Yes, I think environmental protection is really important.

Ich habe große Angst um den Treibhauseffekt.
I am really afraid of the greenhouse effect.

Nein, ich interessiere mich ganz und gar nicht dafür.
No, I'm not at all interested in it.

Es geht mich nichts an. Ich spiele lieber Fußball.
It doesn't concern me. I prefer playing football.

Travel and the Environment

Es gibt zu viele Autos auf der Straße.
There are too many cars on the road.

In der Hauptverkehrszeit gibt es viele Staus.
At rush hour there are a lot of traffic jams.

Wir müssen Autofahrer dazu ermutigen, ihre Autos abzustellen.
We must encourage drivers to park their cars.

Man kann zu Fuß zur Arbeit gehen.
You can walk to work.

Wir müssen das öffentliche Verkehrssystem entwickeln, weil es zu viel Smog und Luftverschmutzung gibt.
We have to develop the public transport system, because there is too much smog and air pollution.

Wir müssen mehr Fahrradwege und Fußgängerzonen in den Städten haben.
We must have more cycle paths and pedestrian zones in towns.

In einigen Städten sind Autos absolut verboten.
In some towns cars are totally banned.

Review making comparisons on page 13 and compare modes of transport.

Straßenbahnen sind... als Autos.	Trams are... than cars.
grüner	greener
schmutziger	dirtier
umweltfreundlicher	more environmentally friendly
besser	better
bequemer	more comfortable
billiger	cheaper
schneller	faster
umweltverschmutzender	more polluting

Using Adjectives as Nouns

Many adjectives can be used as nouns. Just give them a capital letter and the appropriate adjective ending from page 28. For example:

alt	old	→	**ein Alter**	an old (man)
arm	poor	→	**die Armen**	the poor
glücklich	lucky	→	**der Glückliche**	the lucky man

Useful Verbs

*<u>ab</u>schalten	to turn / switch off
garantieren	guarantee
gebrauchen	to use
reinigen	to clean
recyceln	to recycle
sammeln	to collect
schaden	to harm
schützen	to protect
sich kümmern um (+ acc.)	to worry about
sparen	to save
warnen	to warn
*<u>weg</u>werfen	to throw away
verschmutzen	to pollute

* separable verb

❓ Test Yourself

What do these mean in English?
1. **Es gibt zu viele Busse auf den Straßen.**
2. **Die Kleinen**

How do you say these in German?
3. Cars are quicker than trams.
4. I cycle and separate the rubbish.

⭐ Stretch Yourself

1. Say or write in English: '**Man muss die Umwelt schützen und umweltfreundlicher werden.**'
2. Say or write in German: 'You should always turn off electric appliances.'

Weather and Climate Change

The Weather Today

Wie ist das Wetter? How is the weather?

Es ist...	It is...
kalt	cold
warm	warm
heiß	hot
frostig	frosty
sonnig	sunny
windig	windy
wolkig	cloudy
bedeckt / bewölkt	overcast
trocken	dry
nass	wet
feucht	damp
kühl	cool
heiter	bright
herrlich	gorgeous
mild	mild
schön	fine
schlecht	bad
eiskalt	icy cold
stürmisch	stormy
neblig	foggy

Es friert.	It's freezing.
Es schneit.	It's snowing.
Es regnet.	It's raining.
Es donnert.	It's thundering.
Es blitzt.	It's lightning.
Die Sonne scheint.	The sun is shining.
Es gibt Schnee.	There is snow.
Es gibt Regen.	There is rain.
Es gibt Gewitter.	There are thunderstorms.
Es gibt Schauer.	There are showers.

Die Temperatur ist hoch / niedrig.
The temperature is high / low.

Die Temperaturen liegen zwischen 6 und 9 Grad.
The temperature is between 6 and 9 degrees.

The Weather Yesterday

Wie war das Wetter?
What was the weather like?

Es war...	It was
Es gab...	There was...
Es hat geschneit.	It snowed.
Es schneite.	It snowed / was snowing.
Es hat geregnet.	It rained.
Es regnete.	It rained / was raining.

Es hat gedonnert und geblitzt.
It thundered and there was lightning.

Es donnerte und blitzte.
It was thundering and there was lightning.

Die Sonne hat geschienen.
The sun shone.

Die Sonne schien.
The sun was shining.

The Weather Forecast

Die Wettervorhersage
The weather forecast

Morgen wird es im Osten bedeckt sein. Höchsttemperatur 18 Grad. Im Norden Regen mit Gewittern in den Bergen.
Tomorrow it will be overcast in the east. Maximum temperature 18 degrees. In the north, rain with storms in the mountains.

Im Süden soll es neblig werden, obwohl es am Abend sonnig werden könnte. In der Nacht kühl.
In the south it should be foggy, although it could become sunny in the evening. Cool at night.

Am Wochenende wird es überall heiter sein. An der Küste liegen die Temperaturen zwischen 21 und 25 Grad.
At the weekend it will be bright everywhere. On the coast the temperatures will be between 21 and 25 degrees.

The Weather Tomorrow

Wie wird das Wetter?
What will the weather be like?

Es wird...	It will...
regnen	rain
schneien	snow
frieren	freeze
gewittern / donnern	thunder
tauen	thaw

Es wird blitzen.
There will be lightning.

Die Sonne wird scheinen.
The sun will shine.

Die Temperatur wird... sein.
The temperature will be...

Build Your Skills: When / If the Weather Is...

Use **wenn** and **als** clauses to write and speak about what you do when / if the weather is bad, etc. Review **wenn** clauses on page 31:

Wenn es regnet, spielen wir drinnen.
When it rains, we play inside.

Als wir in der Schweiz waren, war das Wetter herrlich.
When we were in Switzerland, the weather was gorgeous.

Mein Hund hatte Angst, als es donnerte und blitzte.
My dog was scared, when there was thundering and lightning.

Wenn die Temperatur im Durchschnitt rund 5 Grad höher wäre, könnte ich jeden Tag eine kurze Hose tragen.
If the temperature were on average around 5 degrees higher, I would be able to wear shorts every day.

Climate Change

Wenn alles so weitergeht (verb)...
If everything continues as it is...

Es wird...geben.	There will be...
einen früheren Frühling in Europa	an earlier spring in Europe
mehr Unwetter im Sommer	more rainstorms in the summer
mehr Gewitter	more thunderstorms
lange Hitzeperioden	long heatwaves
etwa 10 weitere Regentage	around 10 more wet days
Überschwemmungen	floods
Dürren	droughts
Hurrikane / Orkane	hurricanes

Die Temperatur wird steigen.
The temperature will increase.

Die Durchschnittstemperatur wird 21 Grad sein.
The average temperature will be 21 degrees.

der globale Klimawandel
global climate change

✓ Maximise Your Marks

Weave a wider range of tenses into your work. Talk about or compare the weather at different points in time and what people do / did/ would do when the weather is / was / would be bad, etc. This is a good way to develop your work.

? Test Yourself

What do these mean in English?
1. **Es hat geschneit.**
2. **Es wird frieren.**

How do you say these in German?
3. It is cold and wet.
4. It was cloudy.

★ Stretch Yourself

1. Say or write in English: '**Wenn es schneit, liegen die Temperaturen normalerweise zwischen minus 4 und 1 Grad.**'

2. Say or write in German: 'It was sunny but in the evening it rained.'

Global Issues

Endangered Species

bedrohte Arten	endangered / threatened species
der Affe	monkey
der Bär	bear
der Wal	whale
der Dachs	badger
der Delfin	dolphin
der Elefant	elephant
der Fisch	fish
die Fledermaus	bat
der Fuchs	fox
der Gepard	cheetah
das Nashorn	rhino
der Panda	panda
die Robbe	seal
der Tiger	tiger
der Vogel	bird

Es ist nötig, die Pandas zu schützen.
It is necessary to protect the pandas.

Man soll bedrohte Arten schützen.
We should protect threatened species.

Die Eisbären sind vom Aussterben bedroht.
Polar bears are threatened with extinction.

Die Waljagd sollte gestoppt werden.
Whale hunting should be stopped.

World Issues

der Abfall	waste
die Abholzung	deforestation
die Armut	poverty
das Benzin	petrol
das bleifreie Benzin	unleaded petrol
die erneuerbare Energie	renewable energy
das Erdbeben	earthquake
die Erde	Earth
die Erderwärmung	global warming
die Hungersnot	famine
die Kernenergie	nuclear energy
die Kohle	coal
das Kohlendioxid	carbon dioxide / CO_2
der Krieg	war
die Lärmbelastung	noise pollution
die Luftverschmutzung	air pollution
die Ölkatastrophe	oil spills
das Ozonloch	hole in the ozone
die Ozonschicht	ozone layer
der saure Regen	acid rain
das Rohöl	crude oil
die Rohstoffquellen	natural resources
die Sonnenenergie	solar power
der Terrorismus	terrorism
der Treibhauseffekt	the greenhouse effect
das Treibhausgas	greenhouse gas
der Tsunami	tsunami

die Überbevölkerung	overpopulation
der Verbrauch	consumption
das Verbrechen	crime
die Verwüstung	desertification
das Waldsterben	the dying forests
die Wasserverschmutzung	water pollution
die Welt	the world
weltweit	worldwide
die Windkraft	wind power

In Afrika verhungern die Menschen.
In Africa people are dying of hunger.

Man könnte die Schulden von Drittweltländern erlassen, um die Armutsbekämpfung zu unterstützen.
We could cancel the debts of the developing countries to help fight poverty.

Ich mache mir Sorgen um die Erderwärmung.
I am worried by global warming.

Ich bin überzeugt, dass wir das Problem des Terrorismus lösen müssen.
I am convinced that we have to solve the problem of terrorism.

Solutions

Was sollte man tun, um die Umwelt zu schützen?
What should we do to protect the environment?

Gegen den Treibhauseffekt könnten wir...	To combat the greenhouse effect we could...
weniger fliegen	fly less
weniger Kinder haben	have fewer children
sichere Öltanker bauen	build safe oil tankers
Atomkraft statt Kohlekraft nutzen	use nuclear power instead of coal power
die Wälder und Landschaft schützen	protect the forests and countryside

Die Regierung sollte mehr Geld für Windparks auf See ausgeben.
The government should invest more money in offshore wind farms.

Es ist wichtig, dass wir zusammenkommen, um das Problem des Treibhauseffekts zu besprechen.
It is important that we come together to discuss the problem of the greenhouse effect.

Die Energie der Zukunft ist Windkraft, Wellenkraft und Sonnenkraft.
The energy of the future is wind power, wave power and solar power.

Wir könnten eine umweltfreundlichere Verkehrspolitik einführen.
We could introduce more environmentally friendly traffic policies.

Länder und Städte sollten mehr alternative Energiequellen nutzen.
Countries and towns should use more alternative energy sources.

Es gibt heute andere Möglichkeiten zur Energiegewinnung, die kein Kohlendioxid freisetzen.
There are other ways of producing energy that do not release CO_2.

Die Autohersteller müssen mehr Geld in die Entwicklung von Elektroautos investieren.
Car manufacturers have to invest more money in the development of electric cars.

Useful Verbs

*<u>ab</u>schaffen	to abolish
bauen	to build
beschädigen	to damage
besorgen	to provide
bedrohen	to threaten
produzieren	to produce
reduzieren	to reduce
*<u>sauber</u>machen	to clean
schützen	to protect
sparen	to save
verbessern	to improve
verschwinden	to disappear
wachsen	to increase / grow
zerstören	to destroy

* separable verbs

✓ Maximise Your Marks

When giving opinions always try and give balanced answers. Use words such as **einerseits** (on the one hand), **andererseits** (on the other hand) and **schließlich** (in conclusion) to structure your response. When using these words remember that the first verb comes immediately after.

- **Einerseits ist Windkraft sauber aber andererseits kosten Windparks viel.**
  On the one hand wind energy is clean but on the other hand wind farms cost a lot.

❓ Test Yourself

What do these mean in English?

1. **Die Regierung sollte mehr Geld für alternative Energiequellen ausgeben.**
2. **Ich mache mir sorgen um den Terrorismus.**

How do you say these in German?

3. It is necessary to protect the polar bears.
4. Tigers are threatened with extinction.

⭐ Stretch Yourself

1. Say or write in English: '**Einerseits sollte die Regierung eine umweltfreundlichere Verkehrspolitik einführen.**'
2. Say or write in German: 'On the other hand, car manufacturers should invest more money in electric cars.'

Social Issues

Issues in Society

When describing issues that affect society, you will find these words useful.

die Aggression	aggression
der Alkohol	alcohol
AIDS	AIDS
die Antwort	answer
Alkoholiker(in)	alcoholic
der Alkoholismus	alcoholism
arbeitslos	unemployed
arm	poor
die Armut	poverty
die Bedingungen	conditions
Christ(in)	Christian
der Diebstahl	theft
die Diskriminierung	discrimination
Einwanderer(in)	immigrant
die Freiheit	freedom
die Gastfreundlichkeit	hospitality
die Gefahr	danger
die Gesellschaft	society
global	global
die Hautfarbe	skin colour
HIV positiv	HIV positive
die Hungersnot	famine
der Krieg	war
der Lärm	noise
das Lotto	lottery
das Mobbing	bullying
Muslim(in)	Muslim
obdachlos	homeless
der / die Obdachlose	homeless person
die Rasse	race
der Rassismus	racism
die Rechte	rights
der Rowdy	thug
der Streik	strike
ungerecht	unjust
der Vandalismus	vandalism
die Wahrheit	truth

Family Pressures

Wie kommst du mit... aus?
How do you get on with...?

Wie kommst du mit deinem Vater aus?
How do you get on with your father?

Wie kommst du mit deiner Mutter aus?
How do you get on with your mother?

Ich komme (nicht) gut mit <u>ihm</u> / <u>ihr</u> aus.
I (don't) get on well with <u>him</u> / <u>her</u>.

Meine Eltern lassen sich scheiden.
My parents are getting divorced.

Sie ist alleinerziehende Mutter.
She is a single mother.

Meine Eltern haben sich getrennt.
My parents have separated.

Ich werde (nie) heiraten.
I will (never) get married.

Ich will für einige Jahre ledig bleiben.
I want to stay single for a few years.

'Auf immer und ewig' ist unrealistisch.
'For ever and ever' is unrealistic.

Ich werde eine große Hochzeit haben.
I will have a large wedding.

Stress

Zu Hause fühle ich mich gestresst / kaputt / aggressiv / deprimiert.
At home I feel stressed / knackered / aggressive / depressed.

müde / erschöpft / schlecht gelaunt / unglücklich
tired / exhausted / in a bad mood / unhappy

sich mit Freunden streiten	to argue with friends
viele Pickel haben	to have lots of spots
ein gutes Zeugnis bekommen	to get a good report
gute Noten bekommen	to achieve good grades

Supporting the Community

Narrating an event or giving details of an event that happened in the past is a good way to get higher marks in your speaking work. Use some of the following phrases:

Was hast du gemacht, um anderen zu helfen?
What have you done to help others?

Ich habe eine Straßenzeitung gekauft.
I bought a street paper.

Ich habe Zeit mit Oma verbracht.
I spent time with grandma.

Ich habe für Freunde gebabysittet.
I did some babysitting for friends.

You can then develop your answers by adding more details. State what other things people could do to help others:

Was könnte man machen, um anderen zu helfen?
What could you do to help others?

Man könnte…
You could…

Ich würde (nie / gern)…
I would (never / like to)…

sich um Oma kümmern
look after grandma

Obdachlosen etwas zu essen geben
give homeless people something to eat

Spenden für den Umweltschutz sammeln
collect donations for environmental protection

am Telefon für die Samariter arbeiten
work on the phones for the Samaritans

mit behinderten Menschen Zeit verbringen
spend time with disabled people

für Menschenrechte kämpfen
fight for human rights

Build Your Skills: Giving Advice

Develop your answer to a health question by saying what you *would* do *if* something were to happen. Review the conditional tense and the imperfect subjunctive (see pages 31 and 55):

Wenn ich gestresst wäre,…
If I were stressed,…

könnte ich mich beim Fernsehen entspannen.
I could relax by watching TV.

Wenn ich Probleme mit Schlaflosigkeit hätte,…
If I had problems with insomnia,…

sollte ich eine gute abendliche Routine einführen.
I should introduce a good nightly routine.

würde ich mit dem Arzt reden. Der Schlaf ist mir sehr wichtig.
I would speak to the doctor. Sleep is very important to me.

✓ Maximise Your Marks

In addition to using a variety of tenses, opinions, adjectives and time words, try to be creative with the sentence structures that you use. Why not start with an **obwohl** clause, for example?

- **Obwohl ich mich gestresst fühle, bekomme ich gute Noten.**
  Although I feel stressed, I achieve good grades.

❓ Test Yourself

What do these mean in English?
1. **Ich komme nicht gut mit ihr aus.**
2. **Ich bin gestresst und ich habe viele Pickel.**

How do you say these in German?
3. Poverty is unjust.
4. I will never get married.

⭐ Stretch Yourself

1. Say or write in English: '**Um anderen zu helfen, könnte man Spenden für die Obdachlosen sammeln.**'
2. Say or write in German: 'If I were an alcoholic, I would speak to the Samaritans, because they work to help others.'

Practice Questions

 Complete these exam-style questions to test your skills and understanding. Check your answers on pages 94–95. You may wish to answer these questions on a separate piece of paper.

Reading

1 Read the statements below and match them to the headings that follow:

A **Ich bin der Meinung, dass man nicht genug Glas recycelt. Das ist ein großes Problem.**

B **Um umweltfreundlicher zu werden, dusche ich mich immer, anstatt ein Bad zu nehmen.**

C **Wenn man Lebensmittel einpackt, benutzt man viel zu viel Pappe und Plastik.**

D **Mein Vater hat ein Elektroauto gekauft, weil das besser für die Umwelt ist.**

E **Wenn es kalt zu Hause ist, ziehe ich eine Wolljacke an, statt die Heizung anzumachen.**

F **Ich mache immer das Licht aus, wenn ich ein Zimmer verlasse.**

a) Saving electricity ☐ (1)

b) Reducing carbon dioxide emissions ☐ (1)

c) Recycling glass ☐ (1)

d) Too much packaging ☐ (1)

e) Avoiding using the central heating ☐ (1)

f) Saving water ☐ (1)

2 Read the transcript of the week's weather review below and answer the questions in English.

> Guten Tag! Ich bin Herr Fisch und hier ist der Wetterbericht. Gestern hat es viel geregnet und es war stark bewölkt aber heute ist das Wetter ganz anders! Die Temperaturen liegen heute zwischen fünfzehn und neunzehn Grad. Die Sonne scheint, aber es ist windig an der Küste. Morgen wird es im Norden bedeckt sein. Höchsttemperatur zehn Grad. Im Osten soll es neblig werden, obwohl es am Nachmittag herrlich werden könnte. Am Wochenende wird es wahrscheinlich keine Schauer geben, obwohl es donnern und blitzen wird. Vergessen Sie nicht den Regenschirm!
>
> Herr Fisch

a) What was the weather like yesterday?

.... (2)

b) What is the temperature today?

.... (2)

c) What is the weather like on the coast?

.... (1)

d) What will the weather be like in the north?

.... (2)

e) What change in the weather could happen in the east?

.... (2)

f) What will the weather be like at the weekend?

.... (2)

Speaking

3 You are discussing social issues with your German friend's mum. Prepare to discuss the following points in full sentences. Give opinions and develop your answers. Record yourself on your phone.

a) Describe your parents' relationship.

b) Give your opinion on marriage.

c) What have you done to help in your community?

d) What would you do if you were stressed?

(10)

Writing

4 You have been asked to write about your plans to make your town more environmentally friendly. Write about each of the following in German, developing your answer and giving justified opinions!

- What are the main problems with your local environment?
- What would you have to do to solve these problems and why is it important?
- What have you done to help and why?

(15)

5 You are writing a short essay about global warming. You need to develop each point and give lots of opinions. You may also need to use your imagination!

- What effects does global warming have on the weather?
- In your opinion, how can we solve the problem of global warming?
- What will you do to help?

(15)

How well did you do?

| 0–15 | Try again | 16–29 | Getting there | 30–44 | Good work | 45–57 | Excellent! |

Word Bank

The following items of vocabulary from each topic area are only likely to appear in higher tier listening and reading questions.

Vocabulary and Grammar

Home Life and Personal Information

adoptiert	adopted	der Kanarienvogel	canary
ähnlich	similar	leiden (unter)	to suffer (from)
der / die Alleinerziehende	single parent	minderjährig	underage
alleinstehend	single	miteinander	together
angeberisch	pretentious	der Pensionär	pensioner
die Anschrift	address	selbstständig	independent
auf Grund (+ gen.)	based on	selbstbewusst	confident
der / die Bedürftige	person in need	die Staatsangehörigkeit	nationality
der / die Bekannte	acquaintance	treu	faithful
die Beziehung	relationship	der / die Verlobte	fiancé(e)
eifersüchtig	jealous	verrückt	mad
eine gute Tat	a good deed	der / die Verwandte	relative
eine vorgefasste Meinung haben	to have a prejudice	verzeihen	to forgive
		volljährig	of legal age
eingebildet	conceited	die Vorwahl	area code
geräumig	spacious	der Wintergarten	conservatory
das Geschlecht	gender	der Zaun	fence
großzügig	generous	zuverlässig	reliable

School and Work

*absagen	to cancel	die Hauswirtschaftslehre	home economics
die Abschlussprüfung	final exam	das Internat	boarding school
abwesend ≠ anwesend	absent ≠ present	die Klassenarbeit	classwork
Abiturient(in)	A-level graduate	das Klassenbuch	register
der Ausbildungsplatz	apprenticeship place	der Kugelschreiber	ballpoint pen
*ausfallen	to be cancelled	Landwirt(in)	farmer
die Aussprache	pronunciation	lehren	to teach
*aussprechen	to pronounce	der Leistungsdruck	pressure to perform
die Bedrohung	threat	Maler(in)	painter
die Besprechung	meeting	die Note	grade
die Bewerbungsunterlagen	application documents	die Patrone	cartridge
der Bindestrich	hyphen / dash	das Pflichtfach	compulsory subject
Bewerber(in)	applicant	die Prüfung	test
Dolmetscher(in)	interpreter	die Schichtarbeit	shift work
sich entschließen	to decide (on)	Schriftsteller(in)	author
das Ergebnis	result	das Schulhalbjahr	(school) term
erklären	to explain	das Staatsexamen	state examination
die Erpressung	extortion / blackmail	die Strafarbeit	lines
die Fachhochschule	technical college	der Studienplatz	college / uni place
das Fließband	production line	der Stundenplan	timetable
Fremdsprachenassistent(in)	foreign language assistant	der Unterricht	lessons
die Ganztagsschule	full-time school	der Unterstrich	underscore
das Gebiet	area / field	versetzt werden	to move up
die Gelegenheitsarbeit	casual work	das Vorstellungsgespräch	job interview
das Gesetz	law	das Wahlfach	option subject
die Gewalt	violence	das Zeugnis	school report
die Gleitzeit	flexitime		

*separable verbs

Leisure and Lifestyle

die Abstinenz	teetotalism
*annehmen	to assume
*sich (etwas) ansehen	to have a look at
die Atembeschwerden	breathing difficulties
*sich ausruhen	to rest
begleiten	to accompany
die Betriebsferien	company holiday
sich bewegen	to move
die Bewegung	movement
bewusstlos	unconscious
die Biokost	organic food
braten	to fry
das Delikatessengeschäft	delicatessen
die Drogenberatungsstelle	drugs advice centre
die Entziehungskur	rehab
sich erbrechen	to be sick
das Etikett	label
fettarm	low-fat
das Fußgelenk	ankle
geräuchert	smoked
der Gruselfilm	spinechiller
gut durchgebraten	well done (meat)
hausgemacht	homemade
das Kleidergeschäft	clothes shop
das Lebensmittelgeschäft	grocery shop
das Mehl	flour
das Möbelgeschäft	furniture shop
der Namenstag	Saint's day
der Notausgang	emergency exit
der Raucherhusten	smoker's cough
das Rauschgift	drug / narcotic
das Rennen	race
der Rosenmontag	Shrove Monday
das Schauspiel	drama
das Schreibwarengeschäft	stationer's
das Sprudelwasser	fizzy water
die Stimme	voice
die Teigwaren	pasta
umsonst	free
die Verdauungsbeschwerden	indigestion
das Vergnügen	pleasure
*vorziehen	to prefer
wirtschaftlich	economical
würzen	to season
würzig	spicy
*zunehmen	to put on weight
*zurechtkommen mit	to cope with
zweifeln	to doubt

Holidays and Travel

die Anmeldung	application
der Aufenthalt	stay
*aufpassen auf	to look after
sich beeilen	to hurry
bestätigen	to confirm
die Erinnerung	memory
das Erlebnis	experience
das Fremdenzimmer	guest room
die Hausordnung	house rules
die Meeresfrüchte	seafood
der Nahverkehrszug	commuter train
die Rückfahrkarte	return ticket
schäbig ≠ gut gepflegt	shabby ≠ well looked after
*unterbringen	to accommodate
die Verbindung	connection
die Wohltätigkeitsveranstaltung	charity event
die Gepäckaufbewahrung	luggage storage
der Zoll	toll / duty
der Zuschlag	surcharge

The Wider World

abbaubar	degradable
die Auspuffgase	exhaust fumes
der Dachboden	attic / loft
das Düngemittel	fertiliser
*einschalten	to switch / turn on
die Einwegflasche	disposable bottle
die Gewalttätigkeit	violence
das Kraftwerk	power station
die Müllentsorgung	waste disposal
das Pfand	deposit
das Schwefeldioxid	sulphur dioxide
der soziale Wohnungsbau	council housing
die Sprühdose	aerosol can
überschreiten	to exceed
das Unternehmen	company
vereinbaren	to agree
verpesten	to pollute / poison
verschwenden	to waste
verwenden	to use
das Verfallsdatum	expiry date
wiederverwerten	to recycle
die Zentrale	headquarters

*separable verbs

Strong and Irregular Verbs

Verb Table

This table contains a selection of common strong and irregular verbs. Verbs with the same stem follow the same pattern, e.g. **anbieten** follows the same pattern as **bieten**. You can find a full list of these verbs in a good dictionary or grammar book.

Remember that the past participle needs an auxiliary verb to form the perfect tense (past): **haben** or **sein**.

ich helfe = I help but **er hilft** = he helps
ich half = I was helping
ich habe geholfen = I helped

Infinitive	Irregular Present (er / sie / es)	Imperfect (er / sie / es)	Past Participle	Meaning
beginnen	–	begann	begonnen	to begin
biegen	–	bog	gebogen	to bend
bieten	–	bot	geboten	to offer
bitten	–	bat	gebeten	to ask
bleiben	–	blieb	geblieben*	to stay
brechen	bricht	brach	gebrochen	to break
bringen	–	brachte	gebracht	to bring
denken	–	dachte	gedacht	to think
dürfen	darf	durfte	gedurft	to be allowed to
empfehlen	empfiehlt	empfahl	empfohlen	to recommend
essen	isst	aß	gegessen	to eat
fahren	fährt	fuhr	gefahren*	to go, drive
fallen	fällt	fiel	gefallen*	to fall
fangen	fängt	fing	gefangen	to catch
finden	–	fand	gefunden	to find
fliegen	–	flog	geflogen*	to fly
geben	gibt	gab	gegeben	to give
gehen	–	ging	gegangen*	to go, walk
gelingen	–	gelang	gelungen*	to succeed
genießen	–	genoss	genossen	to enjoy
geschehen	geschieht	geschah	geschehen*	to happen
gewinnen	–	gewann	gewonnen	to win
greifen	–	griff	gegriffen	to grab, grasp
haben	hat	hatte	gehabt	to have
halten	hält	hielt	gehalten	to stop
heißen	–	hieß	geheißen	to be called
helfen	hilft	half	geholfen	to help
kennen	–	kannte	gekannt	to know (people)
kommen	–	kam	gekommen*	to come
können	kann	konnte	gekonnt	to be able to
lassen	lässt	ließ	gelassen	to leave
laufen	läuft	lief	gelaufen*	to run
leiden	–	litt	gelitten	to suffer
leihen	–	lieh	geliehen	to lend

*indicates auxiliary verb **sein** in the perfect / pluperfect tense.

Infinitive	Irregular Present (er / sie / es)	Imperfect (er / sie / es)	Past Participle	Meaning
lesen	liest	las	gelesen	to read
liegen	–	lag	gelegen	to lie (on beach, etc.)
lügen	–	log	gelogen	to tell a lie
mögen	mag	mochte	gemocht	to like
müssen	muss	musste	gemusst	to have to
nehmen	nimmt	nahm	genommen	to take
nennen	–	nannte	genannt	to name
raten	rät	riet	geraten	to guess / to advise
reiten	–	ritt	geritten*	to ride (horses)
rufen	–	rief	gerufen	to call
scheinen	–	schien	geschienen	to shine
schlafen	schläft	schlief	geschlafen	to sleep
schlagen	schlägt	schlug	geschlagen	to hit
schließen	–	schloss	geschlossen	to shut
schneiden	–	schnitt	geschnitten	to cut
schreiben	–	schrieb	geschrieben	to write
sehen	sieht	sah	gesehen	to see
sein	ist	war	gewesen*	to be
sitzen	–	saß	gesessen	to sit
sollen	soll	sollte	gesollt	to be supposed to
sprechen	spricht	sprach	gesprochen	to speak
stehen	–	stand	gestanden	to stand
stehlen	stiehlt	stahl	gestohlen	to steal
steigen	–	stieg	gestiegen*	to climb
sterben	stirbt	starb	gestorben*	to die
tragen	trägt	trug	getragen	to wear / to carry
treffen	trifft	traf	getroffen	to meet
treiben	–	trieb	getrieben	to do (sport)
trinken	–	trank	getrunken	to drink
tun	–	tat	getan	to do
vergessen	vergisst	vergaß	vergessen	to forget
verlieren	–	verlor	verloren	to lose
verschwinden	–	verschwand	verschwunden*	to disappear
waschen	wäscht	wusch	gewaschen	to wash
werden	wird	wurde	geworden*	to become
werfen	wirft	warf	geworfen	to throw
wissen	weiß	wusste	gewusst	to know (facts)
wollen	will	wollte	gewollt	to want

Vocabulary and Grammar

Pronouns and Verb Tenses

Pronouns

Personal pronouns need to change when they are used in the nominative, accusative and dative cases:

Nominative	Accusative	Dative
ich	mich	mir
du	dich	dir
er	ihn	ihm
sie	sie	ihr
wir	uns	uns
ihr	euch	euch
sie	sie	ihnen
Sie	Sie	Ihnen

The Present Tense – Regular Verbs

The present tense is used to talk about things that you *usually do* or *are doing now*.

Remove the **–en** to find the stem of regular verbs:

trinken – to drink ➡ stem = **trink** (–en)

Regular verbs all have the same pattern of endings.

ich trinke	I drink
du trinkst	you drink
er / sie / es trinkt	he / she / it drinks
wir trinken	we drink
ihr trinkt	you drink
sie trinken	they drink
Sie trinken	you drink

✓ Maximise Your Marks

Include at least three tenses in your work for an A or A* grade.

Present tense:
- **Ich arbeite als Kellner.** I work as a waiter.

Perfect tense:
- **Letztes Jahr habe ich in einem Büro gearbeitet.** Last year I worked in an office.

Future tense:
- **Nächstes Jahr werde ich auf die Oberstufe gehen.** Next year I will go into the sixth form.

The Present Tense – Irregular Verbs

Some common verbs do not follow the same regular pattern. These verbs change in the **du** and the **er / sie / es** forms, usually changing the first vowel of the stem. The endings remain the same:

geben	to give
ich gebe	I give
du gibst	you give
er / sie / es gibt	he / she / it gives
lesen	to read
ich lese	I read
du liest	you read
er / sie / es liest	he / she / it reads

See pages 84–85 for a list of irregular verbs.

The Perfect Tense

The perfect tense is used to talk about things which happened and were completed in the past.

The perfect tense is made up of two parts:

haben or **sein** + past participle

Ich habe **gestern Klavier** gespielt.
I played the piano yesterday.

Regular past participles start with **ge–** and end in **–t**. Chop the **–en** off the infinitive and glue a **ge–** to the front and a **–t** to the end:

ge + **tipp** + t = **getippt**

ich habe gearbeitet	I (have) worked
du hast gearbeitet	you (have) worked
er hat gearbeitet	he (has) worked
wir haben gearbeitet	we (have) worked
ihr habt gearbeitet	you (have) worked
sie haben gearbeitet	they (have) worked
Sie haben gearbeitet	you (have) worked

The past participles of *irregular* verbs do not follow the regular pattern. These need to be learnt. You can find some of the main ones on pages 84–85.

Ich habe...gegessen	I ate...
Ich habe...verbracht	I spent...
Ich habe...geschrieben	I wrote...

The Perfect Tense – Verbs with 'Sein'

There are some verbs that form the perfect tense using **sein** instead of **haben**. Most of these verbs describe movement from one place to another. These verbs have mostly *irregular* past participles and need to be learnt. You can find these verbs on pages 84–85.

> **sein** + past participle:

ich bin ... ge**fahr**en	I (have) travelled...
du bist ... ge**gangen**	you went / have gone...
er ist ... ge**komm**en	he came / has come...
wir sind ... ge**schwommen**	we swam / have swum...
ihr seid ... ge**wesen**	you were / have been...
sie sind ... ge**stiegen**	they (have) climbed...
Sie sind ... ge**worden**	you became / have become...

The Imperfect Tense – Regular Verbs

The imperfect tense, or simple past as it is also known, is used to describe events in the past (did / was doing / used to do).

The verb **sein** is regularly used in the imperfect to say 'was / were' and the verb **haben** is regularly used in the imperfect to say 'had'.

sein	to be	**haben**	to have
ich war	I was	**ich** hatte	I had
du warst	you were	**du** hattest	you had
er / sie / es war	he / she / it was	**er / sie / es** hatte	he / she / it had
wir waren	we were	**wir** hatten	we had
ihr wart	you were	**ihr** hattet	you had
sie waren	they were	**sie** hatten	they had
Sie waren	you were	**Sie** hatten	you had

To form the imperfect tense of regular verbs, find the stem of the verb and add the following endings.

ich spiel**te**	I played, was playing
du kauf**test**	you bought, were buying
er / sie / es dauer**te**	he / she / it lasted, was lasting
wir übernachte**ten**	we stayed, were staying
ihr zelte**tet**	you camped, were camping
sie mach**ten**	they made, were making
Sie putz**ten**	you cleaned, were cleaning

The Imperfect Tense – Irregular Verbs

To form the imperfect tense of *irregular* verbs, find the stem of the verb in the verb tables on pages 84–85 and add the following endings to the stem given:

ich fuhr	I travelled, was travelling
du ging**st**	you went, were going
er / sie / es aß	he / she / it ate, was eating
wir schlief**en**	we slept, were sleeping
ihr trank**t**	you drank, were drinking
sie blieb**en**	they stayed, were staying
Sie sang**en**	you sang, were singing

The Pluperfect Tense

The pluperfect tense is used to describe events that *had happened* before another event happened. It is made up of two parts:

> the imperfect of **haben** or **sein** + a past participle

Mein Vater <u>hatte</u> **eine Party für Mutti organisiert.**
My dad <u>had</u> organised a party for my mother.

Meine Tante <u>hatte</u> **viele Gäste einge**laden.
My aunty <u>had</u> invited lots of guests.

Wir <u>waren</u> **in den Supermarkt ge**gangen.
We <u>had</u> gone to the supermarket.

The Future Tense

The future tense is used to express a firm intention or to consider decisions about the future. It is formed as follows:

> **werden** + an infinitive

Ich werde Pommes essen.	I will eat chips.
Du wirst Tee trinken.	You will drink tea.
Er / Sie / Es wird fernsehen.	He / She / It will watch TV.
Wir werden Bücher lesen.	We will read books.
Ihr werdet Golf spielen.	You will play golf.
Sie werden laut singen.	They will sing loudly.
Sie werden nach Wien fahren.	You will travel to Vienna.

Pronouns and Verb Tenses

The Conditional Mood

The conditional mood is used in situations where something *would happen* or *would be true* under certain circumstances.

The conditional mood usually expresses doubt or uncertainty and is classed as another tense by examiners, so include it in your work for added complexity and range of language.

You use the verb **würden** to express what you 'would do' in German, with the infinitive going at the end of the sentence. For example:

Ich würde weinen. I would cry.

Wir würden das anders machen.
We would do that differently.

Ich würde Jeans tragen.	I would wear jeans.
du würdest	you would
er / sie / es würde	he / she / it would
wir würden	we would
ihr würdet	you would
sie würden	they would
Sie würden	you would

It is also common to use **ich möchte** (I would like) with the infinitive at the end to say what you 'would like to' do. For example:

Ich möchte als Arzt arbeiten.
I would like to work as a doctor.

You use the conditional of **haben** and **sein** to say:
ich hätte... I would have   **ich wäre...** I would be

Modal Verbs

Modal verbs are useful verbs which are used with the infinitive of another verb. As with the future tense, the infinitive goes to the end of the sentence. Learn to use and recognise these modal verbs.

können to be able to (can)	müssen to have to	dürfen to be allowed to	sollen to ought to	wollen to want to	mögen to like to
ich kann	ich muss	ich darf	ich soll	ich will	ich mag
du kannst	du musst	du darfst	du sollst	du willst	du magst
man / er kann	man / er muss	man / er darf	man / er soll	man / er will	man / er mag
wir können	wir müssen	wir dürfen	wir sollen	wir wollen	wir mögen
ihr könnt	ihr müsst	ihr dürft	ihr sollt	ihr wollt	ihr mögt
sie können	sie müssen	sie dürfen	sie sollen	sie wollen	sie mögen
Sie können	Sie müssen	Sie dürfen	Sie sollen	Sie wollen	Sie mögen

Modal Verbs – Imperfect Tense

You need to use the imperfect tense when describing actions in the past using modal verbs. The infinitive would go at the end of the sentence.

Ich konnte sieben Kuchen essen.
I was able to eat seven cakes.

Wir wollten ins Kino gehen.
We wanted to go to the cinema.

Here is a list of the modal verbs in the imperfect tense:

Infinitive	'ich' form	Meaning
können	konnte	was able to
dürfen	durfte	was allowed to
mögen	mochte	liked
müssen	musste	had to
sollen	sollte	was supposed to
wollen	wollte	wanted to

Answers

Speaking

Marks will be awarded as follows:

9–10 Marks
Very Good
This means you have covered all the points and given detailed answers, including plenty of relevant information. You have spoken clearly, and have included opinions and reasons for your opinions. You have used some longer sentences and you have used more than one tense.

7–8 Marks
Good
This means you have covered all the points but one of the points may not be as detailed as the others. You have given quite a lot of information clearly, and have included some opinions and reasons. You have used some longer sentences and you have used more than one tense.

5–6 Marks
Sufficient
This means you might not have covered one or two of the points but what you have said conveys some information and there are opinions expressed. Most of your sentences are quite short and your answer may not show much evidence of different tenses.

3–4 Marks
Limited
This means that you have spoken in brief sentences and included some simple opinions but your answer lacks detail and you have missed out some of the information you were asked to give. Your sentences are short and you have used only one tense.

1–2 Marks
Poor
This means that you could not really answer the question and that you gave very little information and expressed no opinions. All your sentences are short and in the same tense.

Writing

Marks will be awarded as follows:

13–15 Marks
Very Good
This means you have covered all the bullet points and given a detailed answer, including plenty of relevant information. You have written clearly, and have included opinions and reasons for your opinions. You have set out your work in a logical and clear structure. You have used some longer sentences and you have used more than one tense.

10–12 Marks
Good
This means you have covered all the bullet points but one of the points may not be as detailed as the others. You have given quite a lot of information clearly, and have included some opinions and reasons. There are some longer sentences and you have used more than one tense.

7–9 Marks
Sufficient
This means you might not have covered one or two of the bullet points but what you have written conveys some information and there are opinions expressed. Most of your sentences are quite short and your answer may not show much evidence of different tenses.

4–6 Marks
Limited
This means that you have written some brief sentences and included some simple opinions but your answer lacks detail and you have missed out some of the information you were asked to give. Your sentences are short and you have used only one tense.

1–3 Marks
Poor
This means that you could not really answer the question and that you have given very little information and expressed no opinions. All your sentences are short and in the same tense.

Pages 6–7 Basic German
Test Yourself Answers
1. acht, zehn, zwölf, vierzehn, sechzehn
2. März, Februar, Januar, Dezember, November
3. Mittwoch, Donnerstag, Freitag, Samstag / Sonnabend, Sonntag
4. rosa

Stretch Yourself Answers
1. einundfünfzig
2. sechs Uhr

Pages 8–9 Basic German
Test Yourself Answers
1. Warum?
2. Nein
3. Wahrscheinlich
4. Bis bald

Stretch Yourself Answers
1. Es macht nichts.
2. Meiner Meinung nach

Home Life and Personal Information

Pages 10–11 Personal Information and Family
Test Yourself Answers
1. My mother is 43 years old.
2. I have two sisters and a sheep.
3. Mein Bruder heißt John.
4. Meine Mutter ist Einzelkind, aber sie hat eine Katze.

Stretch Yourself Answers
1. I have a mouse that is called Ian.
2. Mein Stiefvater hat einen Sohn, der sechs Jahre alt ist.

Pages 12–13 Family and Friends
Test Yourself Answers
1. My cat has big, green eyes.
2. Matthew is my best friend.
3. Meine Mutter hat wirklich lockige Haare.
4. Ich bin sportlicher als mein Bruder.

Stretch Yourself Answers
1. She is younger than me and older than my sister, who is quite lazy.
2. Mein Onkel, der Andrew heißt, hat den größten Schnurrbart.

Pages 14–15 Relationship and Personality
Test Yourself Answers
1. My brother gets on my nerves.
2. I love my granny, but she is too strict.
3. Ich kann meine Schwester nicht leiden.
4. Mein idealer Partner / Meine ideale Partnerin ist reich und muskulös.

Stretch Yourself Answers
1. My ideal partner is not only slim, but also rather loving. But I have a big problem: I have loads of big spots and I don't like spots.
2. Mein Halbbruder ist sowohl sehr egoistisch als auch schlecht gelaunt, aber ich liebe ihn.

Pages 16–17 Future Plans
Test Yourself Answers
1. I would like to become a millionaire.
2. We don't want to celebrate the anniversary.
3. Ich möchte zehn Kinder haben.
4. Mein Bruder wird in Berlin studieren.

Stretch Yourself Answers
1. I intend to study German in the sixth form, but my sister would like to marry as well as have 11 children!
2. Meine Eltern hoffen, reich und berühmt zu werden, aber ich will nur auf die Universität gehen.

Pages 18–19 House and Home
Test Yourself Answers
1. The house has a kitchen and two living rooms.
2. I live in a house in the countryside.
3. Ich wohne in einer Wohnung im zweiten Stock.
4. Das Haus liegt an der Küste.

Stretch Yourself Answers
1. ich esse, du isst, er / sie / es isst, wir essen, ihr esst, sie essen, Sie essen
2. einen Tisch

Pages 20–21 Daily Routine
Test Yourself Answers
1. mich, dich, sich, uns, euch, sich, sich
2. A separable verb has a prefix which goes to the end of the sentence in the present tense.
3. Possible answers: Ich mache das Bett; Ich räume den Tisch ab; Ich mähe den Rasen; Ich helfe mit dem Müll etc.

Stretch Yourself Answers
1. Normally I get up early, but tomorrow I will get up at nine o'clock.
2. Jeden Tag kämmst du dir die Haare.

Pages 22–23 Local Environment
Test Yourself Answers
1. I don't like visiting museums because they are depressing.
2. Die Stadt hat ungefähr 70.000 Einwohner und viel zu bieten.
3. Die Gegend ist sauber, aber es gibt viel Lärm.

Stretch Yourself Answers
1. In the evening there is a disco, where you can hang around, although the biggest advantage is that there is also a great amusement park.
2. Im Großen und Ganzen ist die Stadt ziemlich lebendig.

Pages 24–25 Answers to Practice Questions
(See the guidance on page 89.)
1. a) Familienname
   b) heißt
   c) hat
   d) Eltern
   e) Schnurrbart
   f) werde
2. a) He lives in Mannheim, in south-west Germany, about 70 km from Frankfurt am Main.
   b) There is a beautiful old castle, a university, a modern theatre and lots of shops.
   c) He doesn't like living there because it is quite boring and you can't go sailing there.
   d) He used to live by the sea in North Germany.
   e) He would like to live in Switzerland, because it is very green and safe and because you can go riding and fishing there every day.

f) The advantage of this lifestyle is that there is no traffic or noise.
3. Example answers:
   a) Ich heiße Andy und ich bin fünfzehn Jahre alt. Ich habe eine Schwester, die Daisy heißt. Ich bin jünger als meine Schwester. Ich habe kein Haustier.
   My name is Andy and I am 15 years old. I have a sister, who is called Daisy. I am younger than my sister. I don't have a pet.
   b) Ich bin ziemlich groß und schlank und ich habe grüne Augen und braune Haare. Ich trage keine Brille.
   I am rather tall and slim and I have green eyes and brown hair. I do not wear glasses.
   c) Ich bin sehr faul, aber intelligent. Ich bin sportlicher als mein Vater, der wirklich dick ist.
   I am very lazy but intelligent. I am sportier than my father, who is really fat.
   d) Ich komme sehr gut mit meinen Eltern aus, weil sie total locker sind. Ich verstehe mich auch gut mit meiner Schwester, die mir aber ab und zu echt auf die Nerven geht.
   I get on very well with my parents, because they are totally relaxed. I also get on well with my sister, who is however now and then really annoying.
   e) Ich wohne in einem Reihenhaus in der Lindenstraße 30. Das Haus liegt am Stadtrand von Nantwich im Nordwesten von England. Hier kann man schwimmen gehen und im Park rumhängen, aber die Stadt hat nicht viel zu bieten. In der Zukunft werde ich in einer Wohnung in London wohnen, wo es viele Geschäfte und Diskos gibt. Der größte Nachteil von London ist, dass es manchmal gefährlich ist. Im Großen und Ganzen ist meine Heimatstadt nicht so schlecht, aber London ist lebendiger.
   I live in a terraced house at 30 Lime Street. The house is on the edge of the town of Nantwich in the north west of England. You can go swimming here and hang around the park, but the town has not much to offer. In the future I will live in a flat in London, where there are lots of shops and discos. The biggest disadvantage of London is that it is sometimes dangerous. On the whole my home town is not so bad, but London is livelier.
4. Example answer:
   Er heißt Onion und er ist ein Schaf. Er ist ziemlich klein und hat schwarze Augen und goldene Wolle. Er ist sehr reich und hat viel Humor.
   Onion hat keine Geschwister, aber er hat einen besten Freund, der Lammy heißt. In der Zukunft möchte er eine Frau finden.
   Er wohnt in einem großen Einfamilienhaus auf einem Bauernhof auf dem Land. Es gibt viele andere Tiere, die sprechen können.
   He is called Onion and he is a sheep. He is rather small and has black eyes and golden wool. He is very rich and very funny.
   Onion has no brothers or sisters but he has a best friend called Lammy. In the future he would like to find a wife.
   He lives in a large detached house on a farm in the countryside. There are many other animals that can speak.
5. Example answer:
   Ich möchte in der Zukunft heiraten und drei Kinder haben, weil ich Kinder sehr lustig finde.
   Ich möchte auf dem Land in Italien wohnen. Ich werde viele Tiere haben und meinen eigenen Wein produzieren. Ich liebe Italien, weil die Leute sehr freundlich und locker sind.
   Ich werde in der Zukunft Rentner sein und ich möchte mit meiner Frau durch Indien reisen. Ich liebe reisen und ich habe Indien nie gesehen.
   In the future I would like to get married and have three children, because I find children very funny.
   I would like to live in the countryside in Italy. I will have many animals and produce my own wine. I love Italy, because the people are very friendly and relaxed.
   I will be a pensioner in the future and I would like to travel through India with my wife. I love travelling and I have never seen India.

School and Work

Pages 26–27 School and School Subjects
Test Yourself Answers
1. I can't stand chemistry. It's no fun.
2. Meine Lieblingsfächer sind Geschichte und Mathe.
3. Ich finde Herrn Schmidt sehr sympathisch und fair.

Stretch Yourself Answers
1. I can't stand my school because the classrooms are both dirty and old.
2. Mein Lieblingsfach ist Informatik, weil der Lehrer wirklich locker ist.

Pages 28–29 School Rules and School Uniform
Test Yourself Answers
1. You don't suffer from bullying.
2. Man darf in der Schule nicht rauchen.
3. Man muss einen Blazer und eine Krawatte in der Schule tragen.

Stretch Yourself Answers
1. I am totally against the school uniform. In my opinion that is really impractical.
2. Man muss einen blauen Blazer, eine gestreifte Krawatte und schwarze Schuhe tragen.

Pages 30–31 Pressures at School
Test Yourself Answers
1. Although I have problems with the lessons, I get good grades.
2. I'm afraid of maths.
3. Ich habe Probleme mit den Prüfungen und den Lehrern.
4. Die Schule wird um elf Uhr beginnen.

Stretch Yourself Answers
1. If I had no friends, other classmates would bully me.
2. Wenn ich schlechte Noten hätte, würde ich Probleme mit meinen Eltern haben. *Or* Wenn ich schlechte Noten hätte, hätte ich Probleme mit meinen Eltern.

Pages 32–33 Part-time Work
Test Yourself Answers
1. I earn €40 per week. I find the work well paid.
2. With my pocket money I buy clothes.
3. Ich arbeite als Verkäuferin in einem Sportgeschäft.
4. Ich arbeite fünf Stunden in der Woche samstags / sonnabends.

Stretch Yourself Answers
1. I think that the work is very well paid, although I hate the job, because you have to work in the evenings and I find that totally exhausting.
2. Ich arbeite zweimal in der Woche in einer Fabrik. Ich liebe die Arbeit, weil ich gern in einem Team arbeite, obwohl mein Freund mehr als ich verdient.

Pages 34–35 Jobs and Work Experience
Test Yourself Answers
1. I worked with animals.
2. I worked in a primary school.
3. Ich habe als Tierarzt / Tierärztin in einer Praxis gearbeitet.
4. Ich habe drei Wochen da verbracht und ich fand die Erfahrung eine Zeitverschwendung.

Stretch Yourself Answers
1. I wanted to work in a school, but I wasn't allowed to do it. I had to spend one week in an office.
2. Wir haben zwei Wochen in einem Geschäft verbracht und wir mussten mit den Kunden reden.

Pages 36–37 Future Study and Career Plans
Test Yourself Answers
1. Sehr geehrte Damen und Herren
2. Ich möchte mich für...bewerben
3. Ich habe bereits Erfahrungen als...gesammelt.
4. Diese Eigenschaften finde ich sehr wichtig für...
5. Als Anlage schicke ich Ihnen meinen Lebenslauf.

Stretch Yourself Answers
1. I hope to do an apprenticeship in order to find a good job.
2. Ich möchte / würde gern auf die Oberstufe gehen, um Biologie zu studieren.

Pages 38–39 Answers to Practice Questions
(See the guidance on page 89.)
1. a) B
   b) L
   c) F
   d) H
   e) L
   f) B, F
   g) H, F

2. Example answers:
   a) Ich arbeite seit sechs Monaten in einem italienischen Restaurant. Normalerweise arbeite ich sechs Stunden jeden Samstag und ich verdiene 35€ pro Woche. Das ist nicht so schlecht, aber meine Freundin verdient mehr als ich. Ich denke, dass die Arbeit echt anstrengend ist, aber ich mag den Job.
   I have been working in an Italian restaurant for six months. Normally I work six hours every Saturday and I earn €35 per week. That's not so bad, but my friend earns more than me. I think that the work is really tiring, but I like the job.
   b) Nach der Schule werde ich auf die Oberstufe gehen, um Deutsch, Geschichte und Mathe zu studieren, weil sie meine Lieblingsfächer sind. Danach möchte ich auf die Uni gehen, weil ich eine gute Arbeit haben möchte. Ich will eine hohe Lebensqualität haben und das Leben genießen.
   After school I will go into the sixth form to study German, history and maths, because they are my favourite subjects. After that I'd like to go to university, because I would like to have a good job. I want to have a good quality of life and to enjoy life.
   c) Wenn ich Millionär wäre, würde ich zwei Pferde und einen Papagei kaufen, weil ich Tiere liebe. Ich würde auch ein großes Haus mit einem Balkon und einem Schwimmbad kaufen, sodass ich und meine Freunde zu Hause schwimmen gehen können. Ich denke, dass ich nicht arbeiten würde, wenn ich so viel Geld hätte, obwohl ich in der Zukunft als Tierarzt arbeiten möchte.
   If I were a millionaire, I would buy two horses and a parrot because I love animals. I would also buy a large house with a balcony and a swimming pool, so that my friends and I can go swimming at home. I think that I wouldn't work, if I had so much money, although I would like to work as a vet in the future.

3. Example answer:
   Meine Schule ist sehr alt, aber ziemlich groß. Wir haben eine große, moderne Kantine und ein Feld, wo man in der Pause Fußball spielen kann. Das finde ich toll! Meine Lehrer sind meistens freundlich, aber einige sind ein bisschen zu streng. Zum Beispiel ist Herr Moore strenger als Frau Gibson. Meine Lieblingslehrerin ist Frau Bart, weil sie unglaublich lustig und fair ist. Ich lerne gern Deutsch, weil es wirklich interessant ist, aber am liebsten lerne ich gern Kunst, da ich in der Zukunft als Künstler arbeiten möchte.
   Wir haben viele Schulregeln. Man darf keinen Kaugummi in der Schule kauen. Das finde ich ganz unfair, weil es nichts mit unserem Studium zu tun hat. Man darf auch keine Sportschuhe tragen und wir müssen eine dumme Schuluniform tragen.
   Meiner Meinung nach hat eine Schuluniform sowohl Vorteile als auch Nachteile. Einerseits ist eine Schuluniform eine gute Idee, weil sie Mobbing verhindert und weil man morgens genau weiß, was man anziehen soll. Andererseits sehen wir alle gleich aus und ich glaube, dass man seine Individualität verliert. Zum Schluss würde ich sagen, dass ich für eine Uniform bin, weil es fair für alle ist, obwohl, wenn ich Schulleiter wäre, würde ich eine neue Uniform einführen.
   My school is very old, but quite big. We have a large, modern canteen and a field where you can play football in the break. I find that great!
   My teachers are mostly friendly, but some are a bit too strict. For example, Mr Moore is stricter than Miss Gibson. My favourite teacher is Miss Bart, because she is unbelievably funny and fair. I like learning German, because it is really interesting, but best of all I like learning art, as I would like to work as an artist in the future.
   We have many school rules. You are not allowed to chew chewing gum at school. I think that is completely unfair, because it has nothing to do with our learning. You are also not allowed to wear trainers and we have to wear a stupid school uniform.
   In my opinion there are both advantages and disadvantages of a school uniform. On the one hand a school uniform is a good idea, because it prevents bullying and because you know exactly what you should wear in the morning. On the other hand we all look the same and I believe that you lose your identity. Finally, I would say that I am for a uniform, because it is fair for everybody, although if I were headmaster, I would introduce a new uniform.

4. Example answer:
   Für das Praktikum habe ich als Sekretär in einem Büro gearbeitet. Ich habe Briefe getippt und Kaffee gekocht. Ich habe zwei Wochen dort verbracht und es war sehr ermüdend. Meine Kollegen waren freundlich, aber sie hatten keine Zeit für mich. Ich fand die Erfahrung negativ.
   Ich habe einen Teilzeitjob. Ich arbeite zehn Stunden pro Woche bei meinem Vater als Verkäufer in seinem Obstladen. Ich bekomme sechs Pfund pro Stunde. Meiner Meinung nach ist das ganz viel Geld. Mit meinem Lohn kaufe ich normalerweise Computerspiele und Klamotten. Früher habe ich als Babysitter gearbeitet, aber das war zu laut.

In der Zukunft möchte ich als Pilot arbeiten, weil ich mich sehr für Flugzeuge interessiere, und ich habe vor, viele fremde Länder zu besuchen. Ein guter Pilot ist immer pünktlich und zuverlässig, und genau das bin ich! Ich würde nie als Sänger arbeiten, weil ich nicht kreativ bin und ich denke, dass ich ein bisschen scheu bin.

For my work experience I worked as a secretary in an office. I typed letters and made coffee. I spent two weeks there and it was very exhausting. My colleagues were friendly, but they had no time for me. I found the experience negative.

I have a part-time job. I work 10 hours per week with my dad as a salesperson in his fruit shop. I get £6 per hour. In my opinion that is quite a lot of money. With my wages I usually buy computer games and clothes. In the past I worked as a babysitter, but that was too loud.

In the future I would like to work as a pilot, because I am very interested in planes and I intend to visit many foreign countries. A good pilot is always punctual and reliable, and I am exactly that! I would never work as a singer, because I am not creative and I think that I am a bit shy.

Leisure and Lifestyle

Pages 40–41 Music, Television, Film
Test Yourself Answers
1. I love soaps, because they are exciting and romantic.
2. The story was very complicated.
3. Ich höre gern klassische Musik im Radio.
4. Dokumentarfilme kann ich nicht leiden.

Stretch Yourself Answers
1. I sometimes listen to rap music on my mobile phone and I often buy MP3s.
2. Gestern habe ich mir *Jaws* auf DVD angesehen. Die Geschichte ist ziemlich kompliziert und es geht um einen großen Hai, der Jaws heißt.

Pages 42–43 New Media
Test Yourself Answers
1. In my opinion the Internet is totally dangerous.
2. I share photos and music.
3. Man kann Informationen schnell finden.
4. Sie können mit dem Handy simsen.

Stretch Yourself Answers
1. I believe that there are many advantages of new media. First of all you can save documents online. Secondly you can save time with the Internet.
2. Andererseits sind die Nachteile deutlich zu sehen: Junge Leute sind von unkontrollierten Chatrooms abhängig geworden. Meiner Meinung nach ist das Internet wahrscheinlich gefährlich, aber ich surfe jeden Tag im Internet.

Pages 44–45 Clothes and Fashion
Test Yourself Answers
1. Emo children all look the same.
2. I am not interested in matching accessories.
3. Ich trage gern eine Sonnenbrille und einen Hut.
4. Ich bin ein Grufti und wir tragen Schwarz.

Stretch Yourself Answers
1. So that I always look different, I will buy an expensive scarf made of wool tomorrow. In the past I was not interested in the latest trends and brands.
2. Das Leben als Grufti ist gut und ich gehöre dazu. Wir tragen eine schwarze Jeans und lange, schwarze Mäntel. Ich habe viele Piercings und eine Tätowierung, da sie echt cool sind.

Pages 46–47 Shopping
Test Yourself Answers
1. I don't like going shopping.
2. This shop is cheap.
3. der Blumenladen, der Schlussverkauf, der Bioladen
4. Welche Buchhandlung? Jene Buchhandlung!

Stretch Yourself Answers
1. Some people are crazy about the sales, but shopping is not my biggest hobby.
2. Ich kaufe oft im Bioladen ein, weil mir der Preis nicht wichtig ist.

Pages 48–49 Events and Celebrations
Test Yourself Answers
1. Ich feiere, Ich tanze
2. Ich habe gefeiert, Ich habe getanzt
3. Ich werde feiern, Ich werde tanzen

Stretch Yourself Answers
1. Ich habe organisiert, Ich bin gefahren
2. Ich hatte organisiert, Ich war gefahren

Pages 50–51 Sports and Pastimes
Test Yourself Answers
1. I dance every weekend.
2. I often practise the violin.
3. Ich spiele täglich Trompete.
4. Meine Lieblingssportart ist Radfahren.

Stretch Yourself Answers
1. When I was at primary school, I often went to parties.
2. Ich übe seit zwei Jahren Klavier, aber ich würde gern Dudelsack probieren.

Pages 52–53 Food and Drink
Test Yourself Answers
1. As a starter I would like the trout.
2. I don't like drinking apple juice. It is too sweet.
3. Ich esse gern Currywurst mit Pommes.
4. Zum Frühstück esse ich Haferflocken mit Milch.

Stretch Yourself Answers
1. For the main course I ate green beans and a slice of ham.
2. Zwischendurch esse ich gern ein Stück Kuchen mit Sahne. Das finde ich sehr lecker.

Pages 54–55 Health and Fitness
Test Yourself Answers
1. I am overweight and a couch potato.
2. I have a sweet tooth and like eating boiled sweets.
3. Das Gehirn tut mir weh.
4. Ich habe Halsschmerzen.

Stretch Yourself Answers
1. To keep in shape, you should go to training every day, because it is healthy.
2. Ich habe mir die linke Arm und den rechten Fuß gebrochen und es tut mir weh!

Pages 56–57 Smoking, Alcohol, Drugs
Test Yourself Answers
1. It is quite difficult to give up cocaine.
2. I drank my first beer at 18.
3. Ich habe nie geraucht, weil das tödlich ist.
4. Mein Vater ist daran Schuld.

Stretch Yourself Answers
1. I know that my uncle is an alcoholic, but you should avoid vodka at all costs, because it is unhealthy.
2. Es ist mir sehr wichtig, meine Prüfungen zu bestehen.

Pages 58–59 Answers to Practice Questions
(See the guidance on page 89.)
1. a) Silke
   b) Serdar
   c) Daniela
   d) Günther
   e) Günther, Serdar
   f) Daniela
2. a) He is lying in bed and listening to music.
   b) He is so tired.
   c) He bought peaches for the fruit flan.
   d) He wore a suit made of leather.
   e) His uncle had prepared a big firework display and it was really loud.
   f) He will celebrate his 17th birthday in Germany, he will have a barbeque party and he would like to have a tattoo as a present.
3. Example answers:
   a) In meiner Freizeit spiele ich gern Klavier und treibe oft Sport. Meine Lieblingssportart ist Tischtennis, obwohl ich nicht sehr gut in Tennis

bin. Wenn ich älter bin, möchte ich Fallschirmspringen probieren, weil es toll aussieht.

In my free time I like playing the piano and often do sport. My favourite kind of sport is table tennis, although I'm not very good at tennis. When I am older, I would like to try parachuting, because it looks great.

b) Mit dem Computer kann man viel Zeit sparen. Man kann Informationen schnell online finden und das Internet hilft beim Lernen. Jeden Tag schicke ich E-Mails, weil es einfach und billig ist. Manchmal lade ich auch Fotos hoch und tausche Videos und Musik aus. Die neuen Medien haben jedoch viele Nachteile: Viele Leute sind wegen Videospiele und des Internets faul geworden.

You can save a lot of time by means of the computer. You can find information quickly online and the Internet helps when learning. I send emails every day, because it is easy and cheap. Sometimes I upload photos and share videos and music. However, there are also many disadvantages of the new media: many people have become lazy because of video games and the Internet.

c) Letztes Jahr war ich auf dem Nantwich Jazzfestival. Es war sehr unterhaltsam. Nachdem ich viel getanzt und einige neue Leute kennengelernt hatte, bin ich wieder nach Hause gegangen. Es hat jede Menge Spaß gemacht und ich werde den Event nächstes Jahr sicherlich wieder besuchen.

Last year I was at the Nantwich Jazz Festival. It was very entertaining. After I had danced a lot and got to know some new people, I went back home. It was loads of fun and I will certainly visit the event again next year.

d) Nächstes Wochenende werde ich mit meiner Mutter ins Kino gehen. Wir werden *König der Löwen* sehen, weil meine Mutter Zeichentrickfilme mag. Alle wissen, worum es geht. Es geht um Simba, einen jungen Löwen, und seinen Vater. Ich habe gehört, dass die Musik ganz spektakulär ist, und ich kann es kaum erwarten!

Next weekend I will go to the cinema with my mother. We will watch Lion King, *because my mum likes animated films. Everybody knows what it's about. It's about Simba, a young lion, and his father. I have heard that the music is really spectacular and I can hardly wait!*

4. Example answer:
Um fit zu bleiben, gehe ich regelmäßig im Park spazieren und spiele zweimal in der Woche Fußball. Ich glaube, dass man sich bewegen muss, wenn man in Form bleiben will.

Ich esse gern Gemüse, wie Gurken und Kohl, weil ich Vegetarier bin. Ich finde Obst und Gemüse sehr gesund, aber ich ernähre mich nicht so gesund, weil ich süße Nachtische liebe! Ich trinke gewöhnlich Tee mit Milch und Zucker. Tee ist relativ gesund, aber nicht mit Milch und Zucker.

Rauchen ist gefährlich und ich habe nie geraucht. Ich werde es auch nicht tun, obwohl einige Freunde von mir rauchen. Ich denke, dass Zigaretten ekelhaft und teuer sind. Bier trinke ich gern, weil meine Mutter mir letztes Jahr eine Flasche gegeben hat, aber ich trinke nicht so oft, weil ich nicht gern betrunken bin. Ich bin der Meinung, dass man Drogen auf jeden Fall vermeiden soll. Ich bin total gegen Drogennehmen, weil ein Freund von mir durch Heroin gestorben ist.

In order to keep fit I regularly go walking in the park and play football twice a week. I believe that you have to move if you want to stay in shape.

I like eating vegetables, like cucumbers and cabbage, because I'm a vegetarian. I find fruit and vegetables very healthy, but I don't eat so healthily, because I love sweet desserts! I usually drink tea with milk and sugar. Tea is relatively healthy, but not with milk and sugar.

Smoking is dangerous and I have never smoked. I will not do it, although some friends of mine smoke. I think that cigarettes are disgusting and expensive. I like drinking beer, because my mum gave me a bottle last year, but I don't drink so often, because I don't like being drunk. I am of the opinion that you should avoid drugs at all costs. I'm totally against taking drugs, because a friend of mine died from heroin.

Holidays and Travel

Pages 60–61 Holiday Destinations
Test Yourself Answers
1. We like flying to Spain best of all.
2. I am an American woman, but I have a German passport.
3. Ich bin Japaner(in) und ich fahre gern nach Asien.
4. Ich fahre oft mit Freunden in Urlaub.

Stretch Yourself Answers
1. I know with whom I flew to Switzerland: with my old aunt.
2. Ich bin letztes Jahr mit Freunden nach Griechenland gefahren.

Pages 62–63 Travel and Getting Around
Test Yourself Answers
1. We went by ferry.
2. In my opinion the trip was tiring.
3. Wie komme ich am besten zum Bahnhof?
4. An der Ampel biegen Sie rechts ab!

Stretch Yourself Answers
1. My grandad flew to Germany by helicopter. He arrived quicker than me.
2. Steigen Sie schnell um!

Pages 64–65 Accommodation and Problems
Test Yourself Answers
1. We spent three nights there.
2. The room had no balcony.
3. Ich habe im Wohnwagen übernachtet.
4. Ich möchte bitte ein Mehrbettzimmer reservieren.

Stretch Yourself Answers
1. The room on the fourth floor had old bedlinen and the air conditioning was not working.
2. Ich übernachtete in einer Jugendherberge, aber leider gab es keine weichen Handtücher.

Pages 66–67 Holiday Activities
Test Yourself Answers
1. I rented a moped.
2. I want to listen to music on the beach.
3. Vor drei Jahren sind wir nach Italien gefahren.
4. Ich möchte skifahren gehen.

Stretch Yourself Answers
1. On the first day I would go sightseeing and on the last day I want to learn to fish.
2. Gestern haben wir uns gesonnt und danach haben wir mit den Einheimischen geflirtet.

Pages 68–69 Life in Other Countries
Test Yourself Answers
1. Bayern
2. Sachertorte
3. Gesamtschule
4. Bodensee

Stretch Yourself Answers
1. I believe that the German language is spoken by around 126 million citizens.
2. Man kann den Kölner Dom besuchen.

Pages 70–71 Answers to Practice Questions
(See the guidance on page 89.)
1. a) Engländer
   b) Englisch
   c) gefahren
   d) Millionen
   e) Jugendherberge
   f) bin
2. a) He went to the German Alps to go snowboarding.
   b) He stayed there for 10 days with his family.
   c) He went by car.
   d) It was really tiring because it took 20 hours.
   e) He stayed at Hotel Mexx and it was very modern.
   f) On the second day he went to Munich and went sightseeing.
   g) He would like to see Austria.
3. Example answers:
   a) In den Ferien bin ich zwei Wochen mit meinen Eltern mit dem Auto nach Italien gefahren. Die Reise war wirklich lang, aber es hat trotzdem viel Spaß gemacht, weil wir unterwegs viel geplaudert haben.
   In the holidays I travelled to Italy with my parents by car for two weeks. The trip was really long, but it was still a lot of fun, because we chatted a lot on the way.
   b) Wir haben auf einem Campingplatz an der Küste übernachtet und ich und mein Bruder haben uns ein Zelt geteilt. Ich fand das echt aufregend, weil wir bis spät in die Nacht Karten gespielt haben. Der Campingplatz war sehr sauber und es gab ein großes Schwimmbad. Ich war davon sehr beeindruckt.

We stayed in a campsite on the coast and my brother and I shared a tent. I found that really exciting, because we played cards until late into the night. The campsite was very clean and there was a large swimming pool. I was very impressed with it.

c) Der Urlaub hat mir sehr gut gefallen, weil wir viel gemacht haben. Erstens habe ich mit meiner Schwester Sandburgen am Strand gebaut. Sie waren riesig! Zweitens sind wir in viele Restaurants gegangen und haben eine Menge verschiedene leckere Pizzas gegessen. An einem Tag haben wir sogar mit Pizza auf dem Land gepicknickt. Das war total cool!

I liked the holiday very much, because we did many things. First I made sandcastles with my sister on the beach. They were massive! Secondly we went to loads of restaurants and ate plenty of different tasty pizzas. One day we even had a picnic in the countryside with pizza. That was totally cool!

d) Nächstes Jahr möchte ich auf Safari in Afrika gehen und, wenn ich das Geld hätte, würde ich erster Klasse fliegen. Es wird viel Spaß machen, weil ich viele schöne Tiere sehen werde. Ich werde auch ein Auto mieten und Afrika entdecken. Einfach unglaublich!

Next year I would like to go on a safari in Africa and, if I had the money, I would fly first class. It will be a lot of fun, because I will see many beautiful animals. I will also rent a car and discover Africa. Simply amazing!

4. Example answer:
Was für eine Reise! Wir sind im Sommer mit dem Reisebus nach Paris gefahren und es war furchtbar! Erstens hat der Fahrer schon in England den Weg verfehlt. Zweitens waren wir dann für drei Stunden im Stau auf der M25. Auf der Fähre war mir übel und als wir in Frankreich angekommen sind, hat es plötzlich angefangen zu regnen. Zum Schluss ist die Reise ein Alptraum gewesen.

Im Gasthaus in Paris gab es weder eine Dusche noch einen Spiegel im Doppelzimmer. Das Bett war zu klein und die Handtücher waren muffig. Am letzten Tag hat mir jemand den MP3-Spieler gestohlen. Ich war sehr traurig, weil es ein Geburtstagsgeschenk von meiner Oma war. Ich würde nie dorthin zurückgehen.

Wenn ich das Geld hätte, würde ich im Frühling mit meiner Freundin nach Brasilien fliegen. Das wäre ein Traum von mir, weil ich Samba-Musik liebe.

What a trip! We went to Paris on the coach in summer and it was terrible! First the driver got lost in England. Secondly, we were then in a traffic jam on the M25 for three hours. I felt sick on the ferry and when we arrived in France, it suddenly started to rain. In the end the trip was a nightmare.

In the guesthouse in Paris there was neither a shower nor a mirror in the double room. The bed was too small and the towels were musty. On the last day someone stole my MP3 player. I was very sad, because it was a birthday present from my gran. I would never go back there.

If I had the money, I would fly to Brazil in spring with my girlfriend. That would be my dream, because I love samba music.

5. Example answer:
Ich bin Engländerin. Ich bin schon nach Deutschland, Schottland, Island und Albanien geflogen und ich möchte auch noch nach Weißrussland reisen.

Ich fahre gern nach Deutschland, weil es sehr interessant ist und ich kann mein Deutsch üben, aber normalerweise fahre ich lieber mit meinem Onkel mit dem Zug nach Österreich, obwohl ich Österreicher nicht gut verstehen kann. In der Regel fahre ich nicht gern nach Spanien, weil es dort zu viele englische Touristen gibt, aber vor zwei Jahren habe ich ein schönes Wochenende in Barcelona verbracht.

Da Deutsch die meistgesprochene Sprache innerhalb der Europäischen Union ist, bin ich mit meinen Freunden nach München gefahren, um Deutsch zu reden. Wir haben in einer Jugendherberge übernachtet, die sehr groß und sauber war. München liegt an der Isar und man kann innerhalb einer Stunde die Alpen erreichen. Wir haben uns die Sehenswürdigkeiten angeschaut und einen Stadtbummel gemacht. Ich würde sagen, dass ich nach Bayern zurückfahren würde, weil es wunderschön ist und die Bürger sehr freundlich waren.

I am an Englishwoman. I have already flown to Germany, Scotland, Iceland and Albania and I'd also like to travel to Belarus.

I like travelling to Germany, because it's very interesting and I can practise my German, but normally I prefer travelling with my uncle to Austria by train, although I cannot understand Austrians very well. As a rule I don't like travelling to Spain, because there are too many English tourists there, but two years ago I spent a nice weekend in Barcelona.

As German is the most widely spoken language in the European Union, I went to Munich with my friends in order to speak German. We stayed in a youth hostel, which was very big and clean. Munich is on the river Isar and you can reach the Alps in an hour. We went sightseeing and went for a

walk around town. I would say that I'd return to Bavaria, because it is beautiful and the citizens were very friendly.

The Wider World

Pages 72–73 The Environment
Test Yourself Answers
1. There are too many buses on the road.
2. The small ones
3. Autos sind schneller als Straßenbahnen.
4. Ich fahre mit dem Rad und trenne den Müll.

Stretch Yourself Answers
1. We have to protect the environment and become more environmentally friendly.
2. Man sollte Geräte immer ausschalten.

Pages 74–75 Weather and Climate Change
Test Yourself Answers
1. It snowed.
2. It will freeze.
3. Es ist kalt und nass.
4. Es war wolkig.

Stretch Yourself Answers
1. When it snows, the temperature is usually between minus 4 and 1 degrees.
2. Es war sonnig, aber am Abend hat es geregnet.

Pages 76–77 Global Issues
Test Yourself Answers
1. The government should invest more money in alternative energy sources.
2. I am worried by terrorism.
3. Es ist nötig, die Eisbären zu schützen.
4. Die Tiger sind vom Aussterben bedroht.

Stretch Yourself Answers
1. On the one hand, the government should introduce a more environmentally friendly traffic policy.
2. Andererseits sollten Autohersteller mehr Geld in Elektroautos investieren.

Pages 78–79 Social Issues
Test Yourself Answers
1. I don't get on well with her.
2. I am stressed and I have a lot of spots.
3. Armut ist ungerecht.
4. Ich werde nie heiraten.

Stretch Yourself Answers
1. To help others you could collect donations for homeless people.
2. Wenn ich Alkoholiker wäre, würde ich mit den Samaritern reden, weil sie arbeiten, um anderen zu helfen.

Pages 80–81 Answers to Practice Questions
(See the guidance on page 89.)
1. a) F
   b) D
   c) A
   d) C
   e) E
   f) B
2. a) It rained a lot and it was very cloudy.
   b) The temperature is between 15 and 19 degrees.
   c) On the coast it is windy.
   d) In the north it will be overcast with a maximum temperature of 10 degrees.
   e) In the east it is supposed to be foggy, although in the afternoon it could be gorgeous.
   f) At the weekend there will be no showers but some thunder and lightning.
3. Example answers:
   a) Ich wohne bei meiner Mutter, da sich meine Eltern getrennt haben. Ich komme gut mit meinem Vater aus, weil er lustig ist, aber ich komme nicht so gut mit meiner Stiefmutter aus. Sie ist manchmal schlecht gelaunt.
   I live with my mother, as my parents have separated. I get on well with my dad, because he is funny, but I don't get on so well with my stepmother. She is sometimes in a bad mood.

b) Ich denke, dass ich nie heiraten werde, weil ,immer und ewig'
   unrealistisch ist. Ich will zuerst für einige Jahre ledig bleiben, bevor
   ich mir einen Freund suche.
   *I think that I will never get married, because 'for ever and ever' is
   unrealistic. I want to stay single for a few years first before I look for a
   boyfriend.*

c) In der Schule haben wir Spenden für die Obdachlosen gesammelt. Das
   finde ich gut, weil sie nicht so viel zu essen bekommen. Wenn ich älter
   bin, werde ich auch für Menschenrechte kämpfen, weil es sehr wichtig
   ist, die Bedingungen für die Gesellschaft zu verbessern.
   *At school we collected donations for the homeless. I find that good,
   because they do not get much to eat. When I am older, I will also fight
   for human rights, because it is important to improve the conditions of
   society.*

d) Wenn ich gestresst wäre, würde ich mich beim Fernsehen entspannen.
   Ich könnte auch mit meinen Eltern darüber reden, weil ich gut mit
   ihnen auskomme, und sie helfen mir viel.
   *If I were stressed, I would relax by watching television. I could also
   speak to my parents about it, because I get on well with them and they
   help me loads.*

4. Example answer:
In meiner Stadt gibt es zu viele Autos auf der Straße und in der
Hauptverkehrszeit gibt es viele Staus. Das verursacht Luftverschmutzung,
die sehr gefährlich für die Umwelt ist. Das finde ich sehr nervig, obwohl
mein Vater auch Autofahrer ist.

Um dieses Problem zu lösen, können wir viel tun. Erstens müssen wir
alle zu Fuß zur Arbeit gehen. Zweitens muss die Regierung das öffentliche
Verkehrssystem entwickeln, um Smog und Luftverschmutzung zu
reduzieren. In einigen Städten gibt es mehr Fahrradwege und Autos sind
absolut verboten. Meiner Meinung nach wäre das eine gute Idee.

Um die Umwelt zu schützen, fahre ich jeden Tag mit öffentlichen
Verkehrsmitteln, anstatt mit dem Auto zu fahren. Ich habe auch meinen
Vater gefragt, ob er ein umweltfreundlicheres Auto kaufen könnte.
*In my town there are too many cars on the roads and in rush hour there are
many traffic jams. That causes air pollution, which is very dangerous for
the environment. I find that very annoying, although my father is also a
driver.*

*We can do a lot in order to solve this problem. First, we all have to go to
work on foot. Secondly, the government has to develop the public transport
system in order to reduce smog and air pollution. In some towns there are
more cycle paths and cars are completely forbidden. In my opinion that
would be a good idea.*

*In order to protect the environment, I travel by public transport every day
instead of travelling by car. I have also asked my dad whether he could
buy a more environmentally friendly car.*

5. Example answer:
Wenn die Erderwärmung so weiter geht, wird es einen früheren Frühling in
Europa geben und es wird überall heißer sein. Ich glaube, dass der globale
Klimawandel zu einem großen Problem wird.

Um das Problem der Erderwärmung zu lösen, müsste jeder von uns
umweltfreundlicher sein. Ich denke, dass man keine Plastiktüten benutzen
und Geräte immer ausschalten müsste. Wir müssen den CO_2-Fußabdruck
reduzieren.

Ich werde immer eine Öko-Tasche mitnehmen, wenn ich einkaufen gehe.
Ich glaube, dass man die Umwelt wirklich beeinflussen könnte, wenn man
beim Einkaufen global denken würde. Ich habe auch entschieden, in
Zukunft noch mehr zu tun, zum Beispiel Altglas und Altpapier recyceln.
*If global warming continues there will be an earlier spring in Europe and it
will be hotter everywhere. I believe that global climate change is becoming
a large problem.*

*In order to solve the problem of global warming, everyone would have to
be more environmentally friendly. I think you would have to use fewer
plastic bags and always switch off electric appliances. We have to reduce
our carbon footprint.*

*I will always take an eco-friendly shopping bag when I go shopping. I
believe that you could really influence the environment, if we were to think
globally when we shop. I have also decided to do even more in the future,
for example, recycling used glass and paper.*

Index